T0230641

Planning Strategic Interaction

LEA's COMMUNICATION SERIES

Jennings Bryant/Dolf Zillmann, General Editors

Selected titles include:

Berger • Planning Strategic Interaction: Attaining Goals Through Communicative Action

Daly/Wiemann • Strategic Interpersonal Communication

Leeds-Hurwitz • Semiotics and Communication: Signs, Codes, Cultures

Schwarz • Cognition and Communication: Judgmental Biases, Research Methods, and the Logic of Conversation

Segerstrale/Molnar • Nonverbal Communication: Where Nature Meets Culture

For a complete list of other titles in LEA's Communication Series, please contact Lawrence Erlbaum Associates, Publishers

Planning Strategic Interaction

Charles R. Berger
University of California, Davis

LEA Lawrence Erlbaum Associates, Publishers
1997 Mahwah, New Jersey   London

Transferred to Digital Printing 2008

Copyright © 1997 by Lawrence Erlbaum Associates, Inc.
   All rights reserved. No part of the book may be reproduced in any
   form, by photostat, microform, retrieval system, or any other
   means without the prior written permission of the publisher.

Lawrence Erlbaum Associates, Inc., Publishers
10 Industrial Avenue
Mahwah, New Jersey 07430

Library of Congress Cataloging-In-Publication Data

    Berger, Charles R.
Planning strategic interaction : attaining goals through communicative action / Charles R. Berger.
        p.   cm.
    Includes bibliographical references and indexes.
    ISBN 0-8058-2308-5 (cloth : alk. paper)
    1. Interpersonal Communication. 2. Cognition. 3. Social
interaction. I. Title.
    BF637.C45B47   1997
    153.6—dc21   96-54036
                                          CIP

Publisher's Note
The publisher has gone to great lengths to ensure the quality of
this reprint but points out that some imperfections in the
original may be apparent

Dedication

金桂花

My wife, closest of friends and teacher of the Korean way, who has shown me the virtues of planned spontaneity. Thank you, always.

Contents

ৰু ◆ ন্ব

Preface

ॐ ✦ ॐ

This is an exciting time for the field of communication. An earlier era dominated by the study of mediated and unmediated message effects, during which considerable research focused on the attitudinal and action consequences of exposure to messages, has begun to give way to a more catholic purview of the communication process. This more encompassing perspective does not deny the importance of studying message effects, but raises the additional question of how individuals generate messages in the first place. This has led communication researchers to consider seriously the links between cognitive structures and process and communicative action. Increased attention to these communication–cognition relationships has produced two additional consequences.

First, although the earlier era of communication research was dominated by studies that focused on attitude and behavior change as primary dependent variables, in this new era, such variables as message comprehension have begun to emerge. This new focus has promoted, in turn, interest in such significant communication phenomena as communication failure and misunderstanding, phenomena generally overlooked by the communication-persuasion researchers of yore.

Second, the focus on communication and cognition has led, paradoxically, to a more intense focus on social interaction processes. Early, linear models of the communication process that depict sources encoding messages to send to receivers whose job it is to decode them are simply inadequate for describing the complex and dynamic interplay of inference, uncertainty, and action that are part-and-parcel of even the most mundane of social encounters. Equally as problematic are asocial models of speech production that ignore complex interaction dynamics. Such models may be quite appropriate for explaining the communicative action produced during monologues, but they may be very hard-pressed to explain the patterns of verbal and nonverbal action that are deployed during ongoing face-to-face encounters between people.

The theory and research presented in this volume seeks to strike a balance between the internal workings of the individual cognitive system and the outer world of social interaction. Whether or not the theory and research presented in this volume stands the test of time, it is clear that complete cognitive accounts of social interaction cannot confine themselves to mere descriptions of the cognitive structures and processes that are responsible for message production and message comprehension. Explicit links must be made between these cognitive structures and processes and the workings of social interaction. The work presented in this volume takes at least a modest step in that direction.

Many individuals have provided both direct and indirect support in making this book a reality. Kim Kye Hwa, my wife and closest friend, has given me very large amounts of support and encouragement in completing this project. The late Gerald R. Miller, my friend and colleague, always urged his students to take intellectual risks and advance new ideas about human communication. His superb guidance has had a lasting impact on all of us who studied with him. My colleagues at both Northwestern University and the University of California, Davis have contributed valuable critiques of this research over the years. Finally, Robert A. Bell, Patrick di Battista, and Vince Waldron read earlier versions of the manuscript and provided me with a large number of insightful comments and suggestions for its improvement. Of course, any errors or wrong-headed ideas that appear in this volume are not their responsibility.

—*Charles R. Berger*

Chapter 1

Introduction

ᙚ ◆ ᙚ

That social interaction among people is patterned and thus somewhat predictable is an assertion with which few students of human communication would disagree. If this assertion were in serious doubt, trying to discern and explain social interaction phenomena would be a highly dubious enterprise. The patterning of human interaction is reflected by the fact that a very large proportion the everyday give-and-take between people is carried off without a hitch. Among such interactions are the countless successful daily commercial transactions that take place between total strangers, as well as interactions that transpire in institutions such as schools, universities, and hospitals. Even when such mundane encounters involve misunderstandings, disagreements, and overt conflict, the verbal and nonverbal acts that comprise these problematic interactions, for better or worse, frequently adhere to well-defined structures; in short, that social interaction among humans is patterned is hardly debatable.

In contrast to this virtual consensus regarding the structured nature of social interaction is the considerable disagreement over the most fruitful perspectives from which to predict and explain patterns of interaction. At one extreme, adherents to a radical behaviorist epistemology (Skinner, 1953; Watson, 1924) advocate a metatheoretical perspective emphasizing the detection of empirical regularities and behavioral contingencies in social interaction, while minimizing the role of explanatory mechanisms internal to individuals involved in the interaction. At the other extreme are those theorists who feature the role of cognitive processes in the production and comprehension of discourse, and minimize the role of environmental contingencies in the explanation of communicative conduct in general and social interaction in particular (Chomsky, 1965). These theorists emphasize the biological bases of language, genetic preprogramming, and the role played by neurological development in language acquisition. Located between these two extremes are social behaviorists like Cooley (1902) and Mead (1934) who viewed the acquisition and practice of communicative

1

competencies in both individual and social realms as a process involving the interplay between external events and internal mental processes. In particular, Cooley and Mead argued that individuals can attain neither a conception of self nor a sense of social decorum anchored in community standards of conduct in the absence of social interaction with others. In a similar vein, social constructionists have contended that social realities are jointly negotiated by those involved in social interactions (Gergen, 1985).

Although these various perspectives are not necessarily competing, doctrinaire adherence to any one of them tends to propel the researcher in the direction of particular theoretical explanations and methodological approaches to the study of social interaction. At the one extreme, cognitive approaches emphasize information processing structures and processes internal to the individual as potential explanations for observed interaction patterns; at the other extreme, radical behaviorists search for the relevant reinforcement contingencies that might be responsible for shaping such behavior. Methodologically, cognitive approaches direct researchers toward the assessment of mental processes by measuring attributes of attention and memory, whereas behavioristically inclined researchers manipulate reinforcement contingencies to determine whether such changes produce concomitant variations in observed behavior.

Approaching the study of social interaction from either of these two extremes is likely to be less productive than adopting a purview that recognizes the potential importance of both cognitive and social factors in the production and processing of social interaction (Levelt, 1989). Clearly, some people perform better than others while pursuing particular communicative goals in specific social interaction contexts. One potential explanation for such individual differences in communicative competence emphasizes the amount and types of knowledge about social interaction that individuals bring with them to social encounters. Cognitive approaches could explain how such knowledge is generated, stored, and retrieved during social interaction episodes; however, such accounts would be incomplete if they did not consider how individuals' social interaction history affects the knowledge base being utilized to produce and understand action, and how current actions influence the structure and content of knowledge structures responsible for guiding and comprehending the actions of others.

Invoking this social dimension highlights the dynamic nature of human interaction and calls into question the utility of simple, linear information-processing formulations for explaining observed social interaction patterns. The information processing demands entailed by these social dynamics may cause interactants to oscillate rapidly between producing social action guided by well-developed knowledge structures like scripts, plans, or memory organization packets (MOPs; Berger, 1995a; Hammond, 1989a, 1989b; Kellermann, 1991, 1995; Riesbeck & Schank, 1989; Schank, 1982, 1986; Schank & Abelson, 1977) and social action driven primarily by detailed online processing of incoming data, thus producing socially communicative conduct that is at once both automatic and strategic (Kellermann, 1992).

Increasingly, those interested in the study of interpersonal communication processes have elected to view the study of human interaction from a strategic perspective (Cody & McLaughlin, 1990; Daly & Wiemann, 1994; Frese & Sabini, 1985; Kuhl & Beckman, 1985; Nuttin, 1984; Pervin, 1989; Read & Miller, 1989; von Cranach, Kalbermatten, Indermuhle, & Gugler, 1982). The general postulate underlying this approach to the study of social interaction is that in their daily interactions with others, people frequently seek to reach goals by employing a variety of interaction strategies and tactics. Although the great bulk of research reported in this strategic communication tradition has been descriptive, there have been a few attempts to enumerate the goals for which individuals strive (McCann & Higgins, 1988). Considerably more work has been done to identify the strategies people use to attain various goals in social interaction situations.

Based on the seminal work of Marwell and Schmitt (1967), a number of researchers have attempted to delineate strategies that individuals use to gain compliance from others (Boster & Stiff, 1984; Cody, Canary, & Smith, 1994; Cody, McLaughlin, & Jordan, 1980; Cody, McLaughlin, & Schneider, 1981; deTurck, 1985; Dillard & Burgoon, 1985; Falbo, 1977; Falbo & Peplau, 1980; Kellermann & Cole, 1994; Miller, Boster, Roloff, & Seibold, 1977, 1987; Rule & Bisanz, 1987; Rule, Bisanz, & Kohn, 1985; Schenk-Hamlin, Wiseman, & Georgacarakos, 1982; Sillars, 1980). In addition to this work on the compliance-gaining goal, others have studied strategies and tactics individuals employ to reach such goals as affinity-seeking (Bell & Daly, 1984; Daly & Kreiser, 1994; Douglas, 1987), comforting (Burleson, 1994), ingratiation (Jones, 1964; Jones & Wortman, 1973), acquiring personal information from others (Berger & Kellermann, 1994), ending close relationships (Baxter, 1979), and assessing the state of relationships (Baxter & Wilmot, 1984).

Although these studies of strategic communication have yielded a wealth of descriptive data about the strategies and tactics used to achieve goals, there are significant problems with the general direction of this research tradition. These problems are especially apparent with respect to the compliance-gaining literature because this particular strategic communication goal has received the lion's share of research attention. Nonetheless, although the ensuing discussion focuses on the compliance-gaining literature, the problems delineated in this research corpus are germane to studies of other strategic communication goals.

First, and perhaps most important, there has been virtually no theoretical basis offered for the entire research enterprise, although some have attempted to begin to remedy this problem (Berger, 1988a, 1995a; Dillard,

1990a, 1990b; Greene, 1990). Researchers have been content to shift their attention from one social goal to the next and to describe the communication strategies and tactics people employ to achieve the goal of most recent interest. Although a few studies have examined the conditions under which one strategy is more likely to be deployed than another for reaching a particular goal (Miller et al., 1977), the variables manipulated in these studies generally do not flow from well-articulated theoretical frameworks. Rather, they are variables that researchers intuitively feel should affect strategy selection.

This atheoretical approach to the study of strategic communication has yielded at least two extremely troublesome outcomes. First, in an exhaustive comparison of various compliance-gaining studies, Kellermann and Cole (1994) concluded that the various strategy lists generated in compliance-gaining studies are ambiguous to the point that studies cannot be compared. This confused state of affairs is reminiscent of the heyday of instinct psychology when instinct theorists were consumed by debates concerning the relative merits of each other's instinct lists. Second, attempts to identify factors affecting strategy choice appear to suffer from similar confusion. Hunter and Boster (1987) concluded that a single dimension related to verbal aggressiveness, rather than more complex sets of dimensions revealed in earlier factor analytic research, may underlie choices of compliance-gaining strategies, (Kaminski, McDermott, & Boster, 1977; Miller et al., 1977; Roloff & Barnicott, 1978, 1979). Given this finding and the welter of inconsistencies regarding the identifiability and comparability of compliance-gaining strategies (Kellermann & Cole, 1994), it is not surprising that message selection data do not predict either reported or actual compliance-gaining activity (Dillard, 1988), and that situational dimensions ge erally do not predict strategy choice (Dillard & Burgoon, 1985). The central premise of this volume is that approaching the study of strategic communication from a plan-based perspective helps to fill this theoretical lacuna, and suggests more productive research avenues.

Accompanying the atheoretical cast of most strategic communication research is the heavy reliance on self-report measures of strategic conduct. The bulk of research done in this area has placed research participants in hypothetical situations, as opposed to actual interactions with others. Even more limiting is the fact that research participants are frequently given lists of strategies from which to choose. Typically, these lists contain global descriptions of strategies rather than detailed descriptions of action sequences that might be used to achieve the goal in question. The problems with such lists are manifold. For example, there is no guarantee that such lists include all of the strategies that individuals might use to attain the goal in question (Clark, 1979). Because there may be considerable variation in the ways individuals instantiate the same global strategy in their verbal and nonverbal actions, responses to these pre-fabricated lists may be misleading.

Perhaps because of these and other problems, Kellermann and Cole (1994) found a lack of comparability of such lists across several compliance-gaining studies.

In view of the meta-theoretical perspective outlined previously, it is apparent that checklist approaches to the study of strategic communication fail to capture the dynamic properties of goal-directed social interactions. During ongoing social interactions, individuals may modify strategies based on their assessments of the actions they see their co-interactants taking. Perhaps, checklist studies indicate the first strategy an individual might use in an actual social interaction situation; however, this "first strike" view may tell us very little about subsequent strategic action, as interaction sequences unfold over time (deTurck, 1985). It is also possible that the local circumstances of a specific goal-directed interaction might be such that strategic actors modify their strategies before interactions actually commence. Individuals might conclude that the time is not ripe for any strategy to be deployed, perhaps because the target appears to be unreceptive to the influence attempt or because other situational conditions are not optimal for pursuing the goal (e.g., when concerns for privacy are salient and others are currently present).

The limitations of self-reports of compliance-gaining strategies led Miller (1987) to assert: "*If persuasion researchers want to understand how compliance-gaining message strategies function in interpersonal settings—or, for that matter, how any symbolic inducement functions in any communicative setting—they must come to grips with the necessity of observing actual message exchanges*" (p. 474). Miller's admonition is consistent with the meta-theoretical stance taken here: In order to gain a fuller understanding of strategic communication phenomena, it is necessary to consider simultaneously the cognitive structures and processes responsible for generating strategic action as well as the patterns of interaction that are ultimately displayed as interaction participants pursue their goals. To confine one's empirical purview to the narrow domain of the self-report is to guarantee that significant portions of the strategic communication process remain both empirically untapped and theoretically unexplained.

In this regard, it is notable that very little of the research reported in strategic communication literature has been concerned with the degree to which various strategies and tactics are effective in bringing about desired end states. This dearth of strategy effectiveness research may be explained, at least in part, by the heavy reliance strategic communication researchers have placed on self-report measures that, by their very nature, do not lead to asking questions about interaction effectiveness. Interaction effectiveness data must be derived from observations of behavior gathered during ongoing social encounters (e.g., Wiemann, 1977), and collecting such observations has been the exception rather than the rule in this line of research. Finally, it is difficult to defend this dearth of strategy effectiveness research because the "effectiveness question" is one that seems to be at the forefront of many communication practitioners' thinking. Ultimately, such individuals want to know what works.

Because of the theoretical vacuum and the methodological monism of the modern strategic communication research enterprise, a number of fundamental questions about goal-directed social interaction remain to be addressed. How do individuals develop strategies for attaining various goals during social interactions? By what processes are these strategies altered when unanticipated contingencies arise during the course of interactions? How are strategies translated to social action? How can the effectiveness of various strategies be assessed? How is strategy effectiveness related to interaction outcomes? This volume touches on all of these questions, some more than others, and in the process of trying to answer them, no doubt raises still more questions. Nevertheless, the aim of the current presentation is to begin to fill in some of the gaping conceptual and empirical voids that persist in the strategic communication research corpus.

STRATEGIES AND TACTICS

In most discussions of strategic communication, the terms *strategy* and *tactic* are used interchangeably (e.g., Wheeless, Barraclough, & Stewart, 1983). The blurring of the distinction between these two terms is unfortunate, because it is theoretically useful to distinguish between broad plans for social action and particular verbal and nonverbal actions used to realize these abstract strategies at the level of social action. For instance, one might decide to employ the strategy of *reward* to induce compliance from another; however, there are numerous ways in which such a broad strategy could be implemented at the level of behavioral tactics. One might use verbal praise or money as an inducement for compliance; even within the category "verbal praise" there are a very large number of combinations of verbal discourse that could be used to actualize the reward strategy at the tactical level. Moreover, the proffering of money could be accompanied by a large array of alternative verbal and nonverbal action sequences. The money might be handed to the person with no verbalizations whatsoever and a straight face, or it might be given with a smile, a pat on the back, and a "job well done." Both of these tactical sequences are potentially rewarding, but they are quite different at the level of social action. *Strategies*, then, are abstract mental structures that subsume broad classes of action alternatives. *Tactics* are observable action sequences that individuals enact to instantiate strategies in their goal-directed actions. This volume focuses on particular kinds of strategies, namely, plans and how they are related to tactical action sequences.

SOME ASSUMPTIONS

The approach to strategic communication advocated in this volume is predicated on a number of assumptions that are summarized in Table 1.1 and explicated in turn in the following text.

People act on the basis of their interpretations of their own and others' actions rather than on the basis of the raw data that observations provide. That is, observations provided by oneself and others, like observations collected by researchers, must be interpreted before they can become data on which subsequent actions are based (Coombs, 1964; Kelly, 1955). This assumption does not imply that all interpretation is achieved through conscious deliberation. A considerable amount of interpretative work, especially in the processing of interactions data provided by oneself and one's co-interactants, is accomplished outside of conscious awareness. The unconscious processing of another's nonverbal behaviors, for example, may lead to the development of certain judgments about that person, even though no conscious thought was given to making the judgment (Lewicki, 1986; Nisbett & Wilson, 1977; Wilson, 1994). Similarly, unconscious processes can subserve social action. Were this not the case, people would find it difficult to carry out even routine actions, and they would never be surprised by their own actions. Thus, the strategic communication perspective advanced here should not be equated with a conscious information processing view.

Another assumption undergirding this approach to strategic communication is that individuals utilize various types of knowledge to understand the goal-directed actions of others and to direct their own actions as they pursue goals. The knowledge necessary for attaining goals includes knowledge about the goals themselves, knowledge of the actions that could be taken to achieve these goals, and knowledge about the social actors involved

TABLE 1.1

Five Fundamental Assumptions Undergirding the Plan-Based
Approach to Strategic Communication

1. Social actors' actions are based on their interpretations of their own and others' actions, not on the actions themselves.

2. Interpretative processes of social actors are largely non-conscious.

3. Knowledge of goals and plans enables social actors to understand others' actions and is used to guide social actors' actions.

4. Knowledge structures that guide social action are the product of mediated and unmediated experience.

5. Knowledge structures are a necessary but not a sufficient condition for the production of effective social action. Various performative skills also determine the ultimate effectiveness of social action.

in the current interaction. This knowledge can be highly abstract and not tied to the immediate circumstances (e.g., "if you smile at people they will generally smile back at you") or it can be highly specific (e.g., "Pat Smith adores vanilla yogurt"). This knowledge is organized by knowledge structures of various kinds (Fiske & Taylor, 1991; Galambos, Abelson, & Black, 1986; Schank, 1982, 1986; Schank & Abelson, 1977) that are activated by goals.

The knowledge structures that guide goal-directed action are built through experience. There are a number of sources of experience that provide the information necessary for building these structures. Individuals may try to achieve goals and acquire information by direct experience as they go through the process. Acquiring information in this manner usually involves some degree of trial-and-error learning. People may also obtain the information necessary for generating such structures by observing others attempting to achieve goals. Through such vicarious learning processes (Bandura, 1971, 1977; Bandura & Walters, 1963), younger siblings may observe their older brothers and sisters as they attempt to influence parents and other adult figures. From these observations they may be able to abstract strategies that can be used not only to influence their parents but also to persuade other adults. Older people also may engage in both trial-and-error and vicarious learning to acquire the information necessary to build more abstract knowledge structures. Finally, people may use mediated sources of information to generate knowledge structures for subsequent action. The thriving self-help book industry, which offers information on topics ranging from how to ask for a date to how to be a more effective parent, attests to the importance of these mediated information sources. TV talk shows and the stories frequently presented by those who participate in them constitute another potential source of mediated information for building knowledge structures.

Although the role played by knowledge structures is central to the generation of strategically communicative conduct, it is crucial to recognize that in the pursuit of social goals, knowledge is a necessary, but not a sufficient, condition for goal attainment. Certainly, some individuals are very good at devising strategies for attaining various goals. These superior strategists may not be particularly good performers when it comes to realizing their strategies at the tactical level of social action. Some excellent social interaction strategists may have odd vocal characteristics or mannerisms that detract from the content of their communication, thus rendering their verbal messages less effective. Similarly, those with strong performative skills may not themselves be particularly good strategists. Their communication style may be highly effective, but the messages they generate may suffer from lack substance.

This is not to say that there is always a disjunction between strategic and tactical acumen; however, these possibilities demonstrate the fact that an exclusive focus on knowledge structures is likely to lead to an incomplete account of strategic communicative conduct; just as an exclusive focus on communication performance would produce an equally incomplete explanation. Of course, in some domains of human endeavor (e.g., politics), this disjunction is significant enough to produce a set of differentiated communication roles involving speech writers, who can be conceived of as strategists, and politicians themselves, who can be thought of as performers. Similar role relationships exist between playwrights and screenwriters on the one hand, and actors on the other.

WHY PLANS AND PLANNING?

Plans and planning processes have been implicated in the production of intentional action by researchers from a number of disciplines. Action philosophers (Brand, 1984; Bratman, 1987, 1990) have accorded the plan construct a central role in their explanations of intentional conduct. Brand (1984) argued that plans and scripts act to guide goal-directed human action; however, he also averred that these knowledge structures are not themselves sufficient to explain intentional conduct. He invoked the concept of desire as an additional antecedent to intentional action, and argued that desire and intention can be conceptually distinct. Desire is the state that produces the necessity for action, but it is not sufficient for the production of intentional conduct. Knowledge structures like plans and scripts are necessary for guiding action, once it is necessitated by desire.

Bratman's (1987, 1990) discussions of intentional action relied heavily on the plan construct. He argued that people generally develop partial or sketchy plans to deal with the attainment of everyday goals. According to his analysis, it is not rational for individuals to develop detailed plans that involve extended time horizons in their everyday lives because unanticipated events may undermine such detailed plans. In his view, plans are bundles of intentions or intentions "writ large" that are arranged hierarchically. He asserted that plans contain commitments to future action and are not simply hypothetical entities that have no chance of being realized in future actions. The idea that plans necessarily contain commitments to action is controversial because others have argued that individuals can and do generate hypothetical plans that they know they will be very unlikely to enact in the future (De Lisi, 1987).

The plan construct has been employed extensively in the areas of cognitive science and artificial intelligence (AI). Since Miller, Galanter, and Pribram (1960) invoked the plan concept in their account of action production, it has been used frequently to explain both action comprehension, including text comprehension, and action production. It has been argued that the knowledge of the goals that people pursue, and the typical plans they use to pursue them, enables individuals to achieve understanding of narrative texts. Of course, narrative texts inevitably contain gaps that must be filled in by readers to attain comprehension. It is knowledge of goals and plans that enables readers to make these gap-filling inferences. This general idea underlies the design of AI systems that aim to comprehend and produce natural language (Carberry, 1990; Cohen & Perrault, 1979; Hobbs & Evans, 1980; Levison, 1981; Litman & Allen, 1987; Schank, 1982; Schank & Abelson, 1977; Schmidt, 1976; Wilensky, 1983). The plan concept served an important conceptual function in the development of computer-action production systems (Sacerdoti, 1977).

Models of speech production have frequently employed the plan construct to explain how individuals move from intentions to articulation (Butterworth, 1980; Butterworth & Goldman-Eisler, 1979; Levelt, 1989). Moreover, research has demonstrated that in the course of interacting with others, individuals frequently think about the goals being pursued in the interaction and the plans they are employing to achieve their goals (Waldron, 1990; Waldron & Applegate, 1994). Hjelmquist (1991) and Hjelmquist and Gidlund (1984) studied how individual communicator's plans are manifested in conversational discourse. In addition, Waldron (1990) reported that of some 2,273 thoughts that subjects reported having during their conversations with others, 44% were concerned with the goals they were pursuing in the conversation and the plans they were using to attain their goals. Because plans influence the production of speech at levels not directly accessible to verbal report (Levelt, 1989), Waldron's data probably underestimate the degree to which plans guide actions as conversations unfold.

Given the pervasiveness of the plan construct in the theoretical thinking of those interested in discourse comprehension and production, and the evidence linking individual plans to the production of conversational discourse, plans and planning processes are obvious points from which to launch the study of strategic communication in general and, within that general process, the production of goal-directed messages in particular. However, as attractive as these constructs might be for explaining message production in the domain of strategic communication, it is reasonable to ask whether there is any evidence for their psychological reality.

The Psychological Reality of Goals and Plans

Students of natural language understanding have noted the central role plans play in discourse comprehension processes. For example, Green (1989) observed, "Understanding a speaker's intention in saying what she said the way she said it amounts to inferring the speaker's plan, in all of its hierarchical glory, although there is room for considerable latitude regarding the details" (p. 14). In the discourse-understanding literature, there is considerable empirical support for the claim that knowledge of goals and plans influences the comprehension of action sequences and symbolic representations of these sequences in narrative texts. Black and Bower (1979) found that goal-oriented narrative episodes are stored as separate chunks in the memory representation of stories, and Black and Bower (1980) reported that story characters' actions that were successful in reaching goals were better remembered than actions that failed to reach goals. Other research indicates that when people are given information about the motives of story characters before reading a story, they recall more story episodes than do people who are not given motive information; although individuals given motive information are more likely to show distortions in their recall (Owens, Bower, & Black, 1979).

Support has also been found for the notion that the action representations contained in plans are hierarchically organized. When people observe others carrying out their plans, or when people read about others carrying out their plans, more abstract actions, actions that are located higher in the plan hierarchy, are better remembered than more detailed actions nested under the abstract actions (Black and Bower, 1980; Lichtenstein & Brewer, 1980). The latter study demonstrated the superior recall of more abstract plan actions that were based on direct observation of action sequences and narrative text representations of the same action sequences. Furthermore, this study indicated that actions not directly related to goal attainment were less well remembered than actions that were.

The importance of goal and plan knowledge for the creation of inferences in the processing of narrative texts was alluded to previously. Direct evidence for this claim was found in a study in which goal, plan, action, and state statements were either included or omitted before target sentences to see whether the omission of these various types of information would influence the time it would take individuals to read the target sentences (Seifert, Robertson, & Black, 1985). These researchers reasoned that the inclusion of such information would help to fill in gaps and thus reduce the number of inferences necessary to achieve comprehension. The presence of this information before the target sentences should thus speed up their processing, whereas omitting such information should increase the number of inferences necessary for comprehension and thus slow reading times. This is exactly what was found for goal, plan, and action information. When these types of information were omitted before the target sentences, reading times increased; presumably because without the information, readers had to create their own inferences. However, the omission of state information did not increase reading times. These researchers reported high false-alarm rates for goal, plan, and action information, but not for state information. These findings suggest that as texts are read, individuals make goal, plan, and action inferences that, together with the explicit information contained in the text, are represented in memory. These inferences become an indistinguishable part of the memory representation of the narrative.

Abbott and Black (1986) argued that world knowledge organized in the form of source-goal-plan (SGP) units is so ubiquitous that it is frequently used to process narratives. A typical SGP unit might consist of the following elements: Mary hadn't eaten since breakfast (source), she decided to get some pizza (goal), so she wrote a check to "cash" to get some money (plan). Abbott and Black contrasted the recall of sentences reflecting SGP organization with recall for sentences related by simple repetition of concepts (vanDijk & Kintsch, 1983). If SGP units serve to organize memory, recalling one of the sentences in the unit should raise the probability of recalling the other two sentences in that unit. Conditional probabilities of recall showed a large advantage for sentence sets written in the SGP format, suggesting that recalling the goal that a particular character had in a story should lead to recall of the goal's source and the plan that the character used to attain the goal.

Although none of the studies reviewed here directly explored the relationships between plans and the production of action, they strongly suggest that goals and plans are not only represented cognitively but that these mental representations exert considerable influence on the ways in which generic experience and symbolic representations of that experience are understood. Given the key role played by goals and plans in the discourse comprehension process and the fact that a few studies have demonstrated that individuals show evidence of utilizing plans to guide their actions in social situations (Hjelmquist, 1991; Hjelmquist and Gidlund, 1984; Waldron, 1990; Waldron & Applegate, 1994), it is reasonable to assume that mental representations of goals and plans also play an important role in guiding the production of strategic communicative action. This role may be played in at least two ways. First, as this brief review has shown, some world knowledge appears to be organized in the form of SGP units that can be accessed from long-term memory. Thus, when individuals are faced with the task of pursuing a goal that has been attained many times in the past, for example, purchasing deodorant at a drug store, a ready-made, canned plan may be available to guide action (Hammond, 1989a, 1989b; Riesbeck & Schank, 1989). Such a plan would be accessed and utilized with little, if any, conscious thought. Second, given the human capacity for forethought, individuals are capable of generating courses of action even when no specific plan is available to them from a long-term store. Although this process may consume more time and energy than the retrieval and utilization of canned plans, it produces plans that may work. Whether a plan is retrieved from long-term memory or is consciously constructed, the fact remains that it is the plan that guides subsequent sequences of actions.

The general proposal advanced here, then, is that the concepts of goal, plan, and planning go a long way toward filling the theoretical void in the study of strategic communication outlined earlier. Although these concepts in and of themselves do not provide a complete explanation for goal-directed action, they direct attention to the process of explaining, rather than simply describing strategic communicative processes. Moreover, the notions of *plan* and *planning* in particular lead naturally to interaction effectiveness questions. Which plans are more or less likely to achieve a particular goal, and is the process being used to generate plans the best one possible?

COMMUNICATION, PLANS, AND PLANNING

To avoid the potential pitfall of focusing too much on cognitive structures and processes at the expense of interaction structures and processes, the general relationships among plans, planning, and communicative action are explored here. Chapter 2 details specific relationships between plans and social action.

Communication as Instrumentality

Although people sometimes seek to interact with others simply for the sake of talking with someone, which is itself a goal, communication is employed much more frequently as a means for the achievement of various instrumental goals. There are many examples of this kind of instrumentality. Individuals faced with the task of getting from point A to point B may have to seek directions to do so, and individuals involved in routine commercial transactions, of which there are a very large number every day, use communicative action to achieve such immediate goals as obtaining goods, services, and money. Communicative activity plays a central role in the pursuit of such goals as requesting behavioral compliance, changing opinions, ingratiation, comforting, and acquiring personal information (Daly & Wiemann, 1994). However, the importance of communication in the process of attaining these goals should not blind one to the fact that in the normal course of trying to reach such goals, people also deploy noncommunicative actions to reach their objectives. For example, in order to request information from someone in a face-to-face interaction, certain preconditions must be met, and in order to fulfill these preconditions, certain actions must be taken. For example, one must be sufficiently proximate to the potential information provider to have a conversation in the first place, and attaining such a goal would be easier if the information-seeker and provider spoke a common language. Also, knowing in advance whether or not the target has the necessary information very likely would determine whether an interaction would be initiated with that target. Certainly, the actions necessary to satisfy the proximity precondition are noncommunicative but essential.

Communication as an Index of Goals and Plans

From the point of view of the observer of goal-directed action, the line of argument just presented suggests that communicative activity frequently serves as an index of the subgoals individuals pursue to reach their superordinate goals. When we monitor others' conversations as a detached observer, or when we participate in conversations as participant-observers, the communicative action that we process as input may provide some idea of both the superordinate goals being pursued by interaction partners and the plans they are using to achieve them. When we observe an individual presenting various arguments on a public issue to another person, we are likely to assume that the goal of the presenter is to persuade the other person, and that the plan being followed is one that involves the deployment of various arguments. Such inferences about goals and plans are made possible by the fact that communicative action is so frequently used as an instrument for achieving a wide variety of goals.

The previously reviewed literature demonstrating the role played by goals and plans in the processing of observed action sequences and narrative texts suggested that inferences made about the goals and plans of social actors and story characters make action sequences and stories more coherent and understandable. Because the communicative actions of social actors and story characters that serve as inputs for observers are themselves based on plans, the comprehenders' inferencing task is made considerably easier. To demonstrate the plausibility of this point, suppose a comprehender were faced with the problem of understanding a completely random action sequence exhibited by two people in a conversation. The comprehender might be able to generate a potentially large number of alternative SGP scenarios to characterize what is going on between the two people; however, although each of these alternative scenarios might describe a short segment of the sequence, no one alternative would provide a good fit with the entire sequence. Because people do not usually engage in random interaction sequences with each other, although some may seem that way, comprehenders are not usually faced with this problem. In fact, because most social interactants generate communicative action that appears to be based on goals and plans, observers can often entertain a small number of alternative hypotheses concerning the goals and plans implicated in the interaction sequence.

Communication and Planning

Not only is communication vital for realizing plans in action, it is also central to the process of planning itself. There are at least two principal roles communication plays in planning. First, and most obvious, planning can involve more than one person. Joint planning is a ubiquitous activity in social life, and would not be possible without some kind of communication medium. The theory and research presented in this book does not deal directly with joint planning; however, this is an area of inquiry deserving of research attention, and a domain that may require unique theoretical analyses beyond those advanced for individuals.

Second, when individuals plan by themselves, they may engage in internal dialogue; that is, they may develop plans by communicating with themselves. During these imagined interactions, people not only can devise courses of action for themselves, they can also develop scenarios in which they simulate the responses of future co-interactants (Edwards, Honeycutt, & Zagacki, 1988; Honeycutt, 1991). Having simulated these responses, the planner can develop contingent actions to deal with them, if necessary. Using this approach, individuals can anticipate the plans of others and adjust their own plans to counter these plans. Bruce and Newman (1978) discussed this form of interactive planning and devised methods for representing this process. Because internal dialogue may help planners become aware of contingencies that could arise in carrying out a plan when it is put into action, this planning mode is potentially highly adaptive. However, because it is generally not possible to anticipate all possible alternative actions that might be deployed by one's interaction partner in a given context, extremely detailed contingent planning may not be highly efficient, and in some senses may not be rational (Bratman, 1987, 1990).

This brief overview suggests that communication, plans, and planning are vitally linked. Joint planning is simply not possible in the absence of communication, and individual planning frequently may involve communication with oneself. In social interaction situations in which people seek to achieve goals, communication is one of the primary tools by which plans are realize. Without communication, plans to achieve many goals would remain locked in the mind. Finally, observations of communicative action guided by goals and plans give rise to inferences about the goals and plans of those being observed. Here, communication is the medium of exchange between observers and those whose actions the observers seek to understand. Given these interdependencies among communication, plans, and planning, it is critical that planning theorists take into account communication phenomena, and that communication theories aimed at explaining strategic social interaction consider the contributions of plans and planning in the pursuit of social goals.

PROSPECT

Given the dearth of theoretical frameworks for the study of strategic communication, material presented in chapter 2 begins to ameliorate this problem by addressing a number of conceptual issues germane to a plan-based theory of strategic communication. Several critical assumptions are examined, and a set of theoretical propositions concerning planning and plan–action linkages is presented. Chapter 3 examines the individual difference and situational factors that influence the degree to which complex plans are developed. Then, the role that plan complexity plays in action production is explored. Chapter 4 presents an extensive discussion of the *hierarchy principle* and its role in predicting responses to goal failure. Questions addressed in this chapter include how individuals go about altering plans in the face of failure to reach desired goals, and how these alterations impact their actions. Chapter 5 explores the issues of plan and planning effectiveness. Several problems surrounding the concepts are discussed, and studies of plan effectiveness considered. Chapter 6 explicates implications of the plan-based approach for the study of human communication in general, and social interaction in particular. Finally, chapter 7 explores potential relationships between the plan-based approach and communication practice.

Chapter 2

A Plan-Based Theory of Strategic Communication

అ ◆ ల

In this chapter the cognitive structures and processes responsible for the production of goal-directed social action are explicated. Specifically, the focus is on the origins of planned action and how plan-based actions are modified when frequently used or canned plans are not available to guide actions. The role that desire plays in the planning process also will be taken into account, as are the ways in which planning may be opportunistic. The iterative nature of planning and goal-directed action is explored along with the roles that such metagoals as efficiency and social appropriateness play in the generation and enactment of plans. Before beginning these explorations, however, the nature of social goals is clarified, because it is the desire to reach these goals that motivates plan retrieval and plan generation.

THE NATURE OF SOCIAL GOALS

The theoretical position advanced here rests on the fundamental assumption that much of human conduct is ostensibly goal-directed. I say "ostensibly" because as observers we are sometimes incorrect in our imputations of others' motivations; that is, people may appear to be striving to achieve various goals, but actually they may not be seeking the goals we believe they are seeking. Although the fact that we, as observers, may make erroneous inferences about the goals others are trying to pursue does not undermine the fundamental assumption that most human conduct is goal-directed, it is possible that in certain circumstances we may impute goal-directed motivation to others when they are not trying to achieve any particular goal, or at least any goal of which they are consciously aware.

Conscious Awareness of Goals

The issue of conscious awareness is a potentially important one in assessing the viability of the fundamental assumption. When it is said that human conduct is goal-directed, one potential interpretation of this assertion is that individuals are consciously aware of the goals they are currently pursuing, whereas another is that to observers, people's actions give the *impression* of being goal-directed, even if those being observed are not consciously aware of the goals they are seeking to achieve. Certainly, the use of the term *unconscious motivation* implies that social actors may be oriented toward the pursuit of goals about which they are not aware. Outside of the psychoanalytic framework within which that term has been used, it is a commonplace assumption that conscious awareness is a relatively scarce cognitive commodity that can be deployed over a very limited portion of the stimulus field at any given time, and that automatic information processing requiring minimal attentional resources is the rule rather than the exception (Lewicki, 1986; Nisbett & Wilson, 1977; Posner & Snyder, 1975; Shiffrin & Schneider, 1977; Schneider & Shiffrin, 1977; Uleman & Bargh, 1989; Wilson, 1994).

The question of whether the criterion of deciding the "goal-directedness" of individual conduct rests on conscious awareness of goals or on the mere external appearance of purposiveness presupposes a simplistic view of the way in which individuals process and act on information related to goal-directed action. Individuals are not just aware or unaware of the goals they are pursuing. In his studies of action slips, Norman (1981) suggested that when people engage in intentional actions, they may access parent schemata that provide the broad outlines for the routines necessary for achieving a particular goal. These parent schemata, in turn, activate lower order child schemata that involve processes about which the actor may or may not be consciously aware. For instance, if one's goal is to go to the market to purchase some groceries and one must drive one's car in order to achieve that goal, one is not consciously aware of the visual and motor routines that must be successfully executed to drive the car to the market. The child schemata that control the shifting of gears or the action of the accelerator are instantiated and run off without conscious awareness. They may be made conscious by deploying attention toward these operations; however, there are other child schemata, involving the coordination of visual information and motor control, that might not be accessible to conscious awareness, even when attention is directed toward them. Norman contended that people are consciously aware of parent schemata or their abstract intentions, (e.g., "I am going to the store"), but they are generally unaware of the various child schemata that act in the service of parent schemata.

The crucial point is that in the pursuit of goals, individuals may or may not be aware of the subgoals they are striving to achieve. Moreover, as goals are consciously pursued, even more abstract but nonconscious goals may be simultaneously attained. For instance, as individuals consume a meal, they may give little if any thought to the fact that food consumption is necessary for achieving the goal of survival. However, even if individuals are not consciously aware of sub-goals or more regnant goals in a given situation, it would still be reasonable to assert that their conduct is goal-directed, because they are most likely aware of some kind of intention. Furthermore, from the observers' perspective, since most human conduct appears to be purposive most of the time, people generally give the appearance of being engaged in goal-directed action. Thus, from the perspectives of both the internal world of the individual actor and the external world of the observer, the fundamental postulate is plausible.

What Are Social Goals?

Having established the viability of the fundamental postulate, the focus now turns to the pursuit of social goals in particular. How do social goals differ from other goals? Here it is assumed that social goals involve the induction of some desired state in other people. The desired state may involve either mental referents, such as attitudes and opinions, or actions. Thus, the goal of obtaining food for consumption is not in itself a social goal; however, persuading another person to lend one money so that one can obtain some food is a social subgoal, and requesting a gas station attendant to "fill it up" is a social sub-goal that may need to be achieved in order to realize the nonsocial superordinate goal of having a full gas tank. This latter goal can be reached, of course, through nonsocial means, simply by going to the self-service pump. In both of these examples, communicative conduct serves an instrumental function; that is, the goal is not to communicate with someone else: the focal goals are to obtain money, food, and gasoline. Communicative action is used in the service of accomplishing these tasks. It is possible, of course, that communicative action itself might become a goal, for example, talking with another person "just to talk" or arguing "for the sake of argument." Even in these latter examples, however, such communicative activities may be undertaken to achieve such superordinate goals as passing time, assuaging feelings of loneliness, or attaining cognitive clarity (Schachter, 1959).

Studies of Social Goals

It is obvious from the examples just mentioned that the achievement of social goals is frequently critical to the conduct of a host of everyday activities. Ironically, however, there has been little systematic study of the kinds of social goals that individuals typically seek to achieve in their lives. There have been a few attempts to delineate the typical social goals that people, usually college students, pursue daily. McCann and Higgins (1988) asked undergraduate students to list all of the goals they tried to achieve in their interactions with others. Only those goals listed by at least 10% of the sample were retained for further study. Given this criterion, 20 social goals were so identified, including such goals as checking ideas, obtaining information, persuading, getting help, avoiding being alone, and making an acquaintance. A second sample then made similarities judgments among the 20 goals. Metric multidimensional scaling analyses of these judgments yielded three interpretable dimensions. The first dimension reflected a *social reality* versus *sociability* focus, (e.g., seeking information vs. having a good time). The second dimension underlying the judgments reflected the difference between a *focus on the self* and a *focus on the social relationship*. The final dimension hinged on the difference between a *task orientation* and an *orientation toward manipulating the impressions others have of the self*.

Although the universe of social goals investigated by McCann and Higgins (1988) is potentially quite large, there have been a number of studies that have focused on the more narrow domain of social influence goals. For example, Schank and Abelson (1977) proposed the following four social influence goals as part of their text comprehension program's PERSUADE package: (a) acquiring information (D-KNOW), (b) acquiring a physical object (D-CONT), (c) getting power or authority to do something (D-SOC-CONT), and (d) getting someone to do something for you (D-AGENCY). Whereas this list of influence goals was generated through rational analysis, some years later a study reported by Rule, Bisanz, and Kohn (1985) asked respondents to indicate the typical influence goals they pursue every day. Their study found evidence to support the view that individuals seek to achieve the four types of goals posited by Schank and Abelson; however, their data also suggested eight additional influence goals. Among these new goals were: changing someone's opinion, inducing someone to engage in an activity, and persuading someone to change a habit.

Comparison of the McCann and Higgins (1988), Rule et al. (1985), and Schank and Abelson (1977) goal lists reveals the problems involved in developing sensible categories for social goals. For instance, McCann and Higgins found that individuals differentiated between acquiring information and persuasion, whereas Schank and Abelson included information-seeking as a type of persuasion goal. Clearly, inducing a person to provide information is a form of social influence, but it is not the same as trying to alter a person's opinion on an issue; although, seeking information may be instrumental in achieving the opinion-change goal. The issue is whether all social goals involve social influence.

Close inspection of the 20 goals identified by McCann and Higgins (1988) suggests that many, but probably not all of them, could be classified as social influence goals. For example, such goals as persuading others, creating an impression, get a date, getting approval, obtaining information, expressing ideas, learning from others, and getting help all involve social influence processes to some degree. By contrast, such goals as avoiding boredom, checking ideas, being sociable, making an acquaintance, having fun, maintaining a friendship, and expressing emotion seem to be less concerned with social influence. However, one might have to engage in some kind of persuasive effort to accomplish some of them, (e.g., check ideas).

No attempt is made here to develop a useful taxonomy of social goals; although, such a taxonomy would be of some potential utility in directing future planning research. As becomes apparent in later chapters of this volume, both the structure and content of individuals' plans vary as a function of the goals being pursued. A useful taxonomy might be a first step toward developing a theoretical model to explain variations in plan content and structure among various types of social goals. However, because the focal point of the present effort is on planning processes and their relationship to communicative action, issues surrounding the development of a social goal taxonomy are not broached. This is an area deserving future research attention.

Goal Hierarchies

Although no taxonomy of social goals is presented here, there are some general statements that can be made about the structure of social goals, regardless of the type of goal being pursued. It is generally conceded that goals are arranged in hierarchies in which subgoals are nested under superordinate goals (Lichtenstein & Brewer, 1980). Subgoals represent the less abstract goals that must be achieved for superordinate goals to be realized. Thus, for example, people who wish to achieve the goal of changing the opinion of another may feel it necessary to ingratiate themselves to their targets first. In order to achieve this subgoal, they might have to find themselves in the appropriate social situation to begin the ingratiation process. Persuaders may also feel the necessity for acquiring information on the issue before trying to change others' opinions, and they may develop arguments as a prerequisite for persuasion. Acquiring information may involve a trip to the library or seeking information from a person who is judged to be an expert on the issue. Once persuaders are at the library or begin their conversation with the expert, other subgoals may have to be pursued to acquire the requisite information. As the hypothetical goal hierarchy represented in Fig. 2.1 suggests, persuaders may also deem it necessary to ingratiate themselves to the target to be successful. The ingratiation subgoal may entail acquiring information about the target, which, in turn, may imply other subgoals such as asking friends about the target and observing the target. The specific actions necessary to realize these subgoals would constitute *plans*, that is, the means for achieving goals.

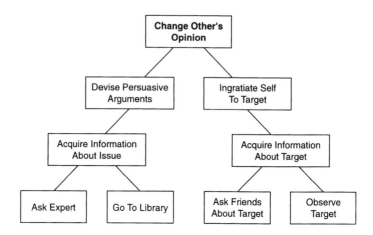

FIG. 2.1.   A Hypothetical Goal Hierarchy

Meta-Goals

In addition to the fact that social goals can be represented in the form of hierarchies is the idea that planning processes themselves are controlled by metagoals (Berger, 1995a; Berger & Kellermann, 1983; Kellermann & Berger, 1984; Wilensky, 1983). Wilensky (1983) argued that the *efficiency* metagoal guides the development of plans to achieve goals; that is, individuals tend to develop the most efficient plans possible. When people develop plans to achieve what are essentially nonsocial goals, this metagoal may assume primary importance. Thus, when a person develops a plan to get from point A to point B, all other things being equal, the person will search for the route that represents the shortest distance between the two points. In this case, invoking the efficiency metagoal seems to be quite appropriate; however, when it comes to social goals, the efficiency metagoal may not provide a completely adequate criterion for either plan selection or plan formulation. In social interactions, the additional metagoal of *social appropriateness* may assume at least equal if not predominant importance (Berger & Kellermann, 1983, 1989, 1994; Kellermann & Berger, 1984). Although the term *social appropriateness* is used here, such terms as *saving face* (Goffman, 1959) and *politeness* (Brown & Levinson, 1978, 1987) also have been used to describe this metagoal. With reference to social action plans, it is most likely the case that the social appropriateness metagoal constrains the efficiency goal. As a result, people establish a level of social appropriateness, and then develop the most efficient plan they can within those defined limits. Thus, for example, in many social interaction contexts where social influence goals are at stake, social appropriateness considerations may rule out the use of particularly efficient but coercive means for achieving persuasion or behavioral compliance.

Goal Dynamics

It is important to recognize that social goals and the values assigned to the efficiency and appropriateness metagoals may change considerably over the course of social interactions. In the realm of social goals, people may see that they will be unable to achieve their primary goal in the encounter and abandon the goal, or individuals may enter interactions with a primary goal in mind, but they may find that they are able to attain another goal. For example, a person may enter an interaction with the goal of creating a friendship but end up becoming a lover to the target person instead. There is, of course, the possibility that individuals will forget their primary goal in the interaction; they may not be able to remember why they initiated the particular encounter (Norman, 1981; Reason, 1990). Not only can social goals change during the course of social episodes, but metagoals may change as well. Considerable evidence suggests that when individuals initiate influence attempts, their initial behavior tends to be positive and polite; however, the longer they encounter resistance from their partner, the more coercive they are likely to become (Berger & Jordan, 1991, 1992; deTurck, 1985, 1987; Goodstadt & Kipnis, 1970; Hirokawa, Mickey, & Miura, 1991; Instone, Major, & Bunker, 1983; Kipnis & Consentino, 1969). In terms of the present discussion, the social appropriateness metagoal appears to assume less importance, at least up to a point, as resistance to influence is encountered.

Goal Multiplicity

Not only are social goals and metagoals dynamic within any social encounter, individuals may pursue multiple goals simultaneously in their interactions with others (Tracy & Coupland, 1990; Tracy & Moran, 1983). For example, in attempting to persuade another who happens to be a friend, interactants must take into account the twin goals of persuasion and friendship maintenance, assuming, of course, that there is a desire to maintain the friendship. Although it is a truism to assert that people frequently pursue multiple goals simultaneously during their interactions with others, it is also the case that frequently one goal serves as a focal point around which the encounter is organized, whereas other goals assume secondary importance. Furthermore, the relative prepotency of these goals may change over the course of the interaction. Friendship maintenance initially might be the focus of the interaction between friends; however, as the interaction progresses, opinion change might become the focal goal and disagreement over the issue being discussed ends up undermineing the friendship.

In this section, a number of issues surrounding the social goal construct have been addressed. Neither a theory nor a taxonomy of social goals was presented. Both of these goals remain to be accomplished. The fact that no theory of goals exists does not obviate the theory and research on plans and planning described in the remainder of this book, because this theory and research takes goals as givens. Providing social actors goals for which to plan and achieve during interactions finesses a number of the issues raised in the discussion of goals just presented; however, the question of how goals arise and change over the course of social encounters eventually must be answered to achieve a complete account of strategic communicative action. For now, however, the more modest pursuit of developing a theory of planning that is appropriate for explaining action directed toward the achievement of social goals is undertaken.

A THEORY OF PLANNING

Why approach the explanation of goal-directed conduct from the perspective of a planning theory? The answer to this question is quite straightforward. Humans are uniquely endowed with the ability to engage in conscious forethought; they may choose to use or not to use this capability in a given set of circumstances. In many instances, there are distinct advantages to employing this ability as one performs a particular goal-directed action sequence. When developing future plans, one may be able to anticipate the potential responses of one's interaction partner and thus rehearse counter-\responses that could facilitate goal achievement. Moreover, when one is in the heat of interaction, situational demands may make it difficult to carry out detailed conscious planning.

Although engaging in such forethought is an *intrapersonal* phenomenon, there is a distinct *interpersonal* aspect to individual planning processes. Specifically, having plans makes interpersonal coordination possible (Bratman, 1987, 1990). Thus, if I know my wife intends to go to a class this evening and needs the car to do so, I can formulate my plans in such a way that the car is available for her use, and I can use alternative means of transportation if they are required. When people have stable plans that are mutually understood, the amount of uncertainty in their relationship is reduced. The absence of plans or the development of unstable plans, by contrast, gives rise to increased uncertainty and decreased levels of interpersonal coordination (Berger, 1979, 1987, 1988b, 1995b; Berger & Bradac, 1982; Berger & Calabrese, 1975; Berger & Gudykunst, 1991).

Given this rationale, the remainder of this chapter is devoted to an explication of a theory of planning. Consideration is first given to the differences between the concepts of *plan* and *planning*. Then, the following questions are addressed in turn: (a) Where do plans come from? (b) How are they formulated when there are none? (c) What happens when plans are thwarted? (d) What governs the selection of plan options? (e) What role does opportunism play in planning? (f) How do physical and mental effort influence planning and plan selection? and (g) How can the effectiveness of plans be determined? The answers to these questions provide the basic outline of the theory.

Plans and Planning

Because the concepts of plans and planning are frequently confused, definitions of each term are advanced to clarify the differences between them.

What are plans?   The following definitions of the plan construct are among several that have been posited by a variety of theorists:

> A *Plan* is any hierarchical process in the organism that can control the order in which a sequence of operations is to be performed...Moreover, we also use the term *Plan* to designate a rough sketch of some course of action, just as major topic headings in an outline, as well as the detailed specification of every detailed operation. (Miller, Galanter, & Pribram, 1960, pp. 16-17)

> A plan is made up of general information about how actors achieve goals. A plan explains how a given state or event was prerequisite for, or derivative from, another state or event...Plans describe the set of choices that a person has when he sets out to accomplish a goal...A plan is a series of projected actions to realize a goal. (Schank & Abelson, 1977, pp. 70-71)

> Plans, so understood, are intentions writ large. They share the properties of intentions recently noted: they resist reconsideration, and in that sense have inertia; they are conduct controllers, not merely potential conduct influencers; and they provide crucial inputs for further practical reasoning and planning...our plans are typically *partial*...our plans typically have a *hierarchical structure*. (Bratman, 1987, p. 29)

> A plan specifies the actions that are necessary for the attainment of a goal or several goals. Plans vary in their levels of abstraction. Highly abstract plans can spawn more detailed ones. Plans can contain alternative paths for goal attainment from which the social actor can choose. (Berger, 1988a, p. 96)

These definitions converge on the notion that plans are hierarchical cognitive representations of goal-directed action sequences. Plans are not the action sequences themselves, but are mental representations of action sequences. All of the definitions agree that these cognitive representations of action sequences can be formulated at a number of different levels of abstraction. For example, a highly abstract action unit in a persuasion plan might be "Offer a reward"; whereas, a more concrete way to represent this broad action class might be something like "Offer $5.00" or "Offer a ride in the Porsche." Finally, all of the definitions emphasize the idea that plans may contain alternative action sequences for attaining goals, and that actors may be faced with making choices among alternatives.

What is planning? In general, planning is viewed as a process that produces a plan as its end product, as the following definitions suggest:

> Planning refers to formulating an intended course of action aimed at achieving some goal... (Hayes-Roth & Hayes-Roth, 1979, p.1)
>
> Planning concerns the process by which people select a course of action—deciding what they want, formulating and revising plans, dealing with problems and adversity, making choices, and eventually performing some action. (Wilensky, 1983)
>
> Planning includes assessing a situation, deciding what goals to pursue, creating plans to secure these goals, and executing plans. (Wilensky, 1983, p. 5)

As these definitions demonstrate, planning is a multistaged process that produces a plan to be implemented in action. Notice too that situational assessment and goal selection are included as steps in the planning process. Recall from the previous discussion of social goals that the present theory does not deal with the problem of goal selection; rather, it is assumed that the social actor has already decided what goal or goals will be pursued in the interaction. The present theory does acknowledge the fact that goals can and do arise during social interactions; however, it makes no attempt to explain these processes. Thus, the present effort deals with the planning steps: formulating and revising plans, dealing with problems and adversity, making choices, and performing actions.

The Genesis of Plans

Given a social goal or goals to be attained, the claim is that the social actor has at least two potential sources from which to derive a plan: (a) a long-term memory, and (b) current information inputs. However, when a social actor is confronted with achieving a goal, these two sources of plan knowledge are not utilized equally; therefore, it is postulated that:

> *Proposition 1:* When persons derive plans to reach goals, their first priority is to access long-term memory to determine whether an already-formulated or canned plan is available for use.

Canned plans are ones that either have been enacted numerous times or mentally rehearsed in the past. Proposition 1 rests on the widely accepted postulates that individuals: (a) have a general tendency to expend as little effort as possible in processing information (Fiske & Taylor, 1984, 1991), and (b) have significant cognitive processing limitations that interfere with their heeding and processing large amounts of relevant data when making decisions and judgments (Hogarth, 1980; Kahneman, Slovic, & Tversky, 1982; Kunda & Nisbett, 1986; Nisbett & Ross, 1980). It is less taxing to retrieve plans from long-term memory than it is to formulate them consciously either before the interaction commences or online as the interaction takes place. This proposition is consistent with the hypothesis entertained by some AI researchers that individuals will search for stored experiences that remind them of current situations in order to achieve an understanding of their current situation (Hammond, 1989a, 1989b; Riesbeck & Schank, 1989; Schank, 1982, 1986); although, Schank's (1982) model contains the claim that such reminding experiences are driven by memory failures.

A corollary that follows from Proposition 1 asserts:

> Corollary 1: When individuals fail to find canned plans in long-term memory, they will resort to formulating plans in working memory utilizing potentially relevant plans from a long-term store, from current information inputs, or both.

The degree of similarity between the desired goal state and canned plans determines the extent to which the process outlined in Corollary 1 needs to be invoked; that is, if there is a very close fit between the desired goal state and canned plans, then a minimal amount of modification needs to be done by accessing other relevant plans or by integrating current information inputs via a working memory. When the fit is not good, however, the planner is forced to search memory and current experience to formulate a plan. This process is both energy and time consuming and is most probably reserved for goals that have a relatively high priority for the actor. Given the assumption that no two experiences are identical, then the notion of a canned plan is somewhat misleading because plans that have been used in the past cannot be expected to match the current situation perfectly. Although this is a theoretical possibility, because of the cognitive processing limitations cited earlier, people probably overgeneralize similarity when the fit between canned plans and the current situation is relatively close. Individuals may be prone to overlook subtle differences between their canned plans and the current exigencies entailed by the social context.

Plan Formulation

Top-Down and Bottom-Up Planning. When canned plans are not available, individuals must create plans to attain their goals. As argued previously, this process is both time and energy intensive; consequently, it is avoided when at all possible. Nevertheless, it is a critical process because canned plans themselves had to be formulated by employing these resource-consuming processes at an earlier point in time. There are two extreme views of the plan generation process. The top-down view argues that plans are first formulated at relatively high levels of abstraction. Action details are then filled in at progressively lower levels of abstraction until concrete courses of action are generated. This approach to planning was embodied in Sacerdoti's (1977) program (NOAH) designed to guide a robot arm. At the other extreme, the bottom-up approach posits that people process action as it unfolds, and from these data derive more abstract plans. This inductive approach to planning has been called bottom-up or opportunistic planning (Hayes-Roth, 1980; Hayes-Roth & Hayes-Roth, 1979).

Newell (1978) made similar distinctions within the domain of motor control. According to his analysis, open-loop motor control requires that initial plans be quite detailed and generally not subject to modification by environmental perturbations. By contrast, the more flexible closed-loop approach advances the notion that initial plans may not be very well formulated and may be modified as the action sequence progresses. Newell argued that the closed-loop model probably is more plausible in the motor control domain. Hayes-Roth (1980) and Hayes-Roth and Hayes-Roth (1979) contended that although planning sometimes may occur in top–down fashion, more often planning is opportunistic, although not completely data-driven.

In contrast to the two extreme positions is one advocated by Bratman (1987, 1990). He argued that it is more rational for humans to formulate plans only partially because future events that might alter plans cannot be predicted completely. Thus, as the planning horizon increases, it becomes progressively less functional to develop detailed action plans because of the increased likelihood of occurrence of unanticipated, plan-thwarting events. Because hierarchically organized plans allow for the development of a number of more specific alternative behavioral instantiations of abstract actions through time, "partial, hierarchically structured plans for the future provide our compromise solution." (Bratman, 1987, p. 30).

Contingent Planning.   Although Bratman's compromise solution is plausible, there are certain possibilities he ignored that call into question the generality of his position. For example, as part of their detailed plans, individuals may not only lay out a specific course of action, they may also anticipate events that might interfere with the successful completion of their plan, and thus explicitly plan for these contingencies. In response to this possibility, one might defend the partial plan thesis by arguing that people cannot possibly anticipate all contingencies that might arise in the future; therefore, it is more functional to develop partial plans. Although it is certainly the case that all contingencies cannot be anticipated when plans are formulated, it is also true that many contingencies have such a low probability of occurrence that it is not worth planning for them. For instance, in devising a plan to persuade an avowed pacifist to change his or her position on an issue, it would not be very useful to consider what one might do if the pacifist were to draw a gun and threaten one in the middle of the persuasion episode, even though it is possible for individuals to display radical changes in both their attitudes and actions. Or, my plans to go to the library to secure a book most likely need not anticipate the possibility that a large asteroid will strike the earth somewhere between my house and the library during the time I will be in transit to and from the library.

Individuals can develop detailed plans that include subplans to be deployed if high probability, plan-thwarting events occur. Of course, one important contingent response that is always available to planners is to abandon pursuit of their goal or goals in the event of goal blockage; nevertheless, as the number of contingencies included in a plan increases, the plan, by default, becomes more complex. Under some circumstances, detailed contingent planning may be a preferable alternative to filling in partially formulated plans as those plans are carried out.

Desire and Plan Complexity. It is important to clarify two different meanings of plan complexity that emerge from the previous discussion. One meaning refers to the *level of detail* at which planning occurs. Plans may consist of a few abstract steps or they may contain detailed behavioral descriptions of the concrete actions to be taken to realize the plan. In planning to achieve social goals, planners can and sometimes do go to the extreme of generating and rehearsing the precise words that will be uttered during an interaction. Such an extreme level of planning obviously would produce a very complex plan.

A second meaning of complexity concerns the *number of contingencies* that plans include. As the number of contingencies included in a plan increases, the plan becomes more complex by default. In the following theoretical proposition the construct of complexity embodies both senses of the term:

Proposition 2: As the desire to reach a social goal increases, the complexity with which plans are formulated also tends to increase.

The use of the term *desire* in Proposition 2 deserves further comment. Some have argued that desiring to bring about a state of affairs, that is, desiring to reach a goal, is a species of intention (Sellars, 1966). By contrast, others contend that desiring can be separated from intention. In advancing this claim, Brand (1984) argued: "A desire can be satisfied by luck or through the efforts of other persons, as well as through one's own efforts. But an intention is fulfilled only if the agent contributes in some essential way to the end-state" (p. 124).

Brand cited several differences between desiring and intending that support the thesis that the two are independent; for example, desire can vary with respect to strength but intending cannot, and the strength of desire can change over time, whereas the strength of intending cannot. This distinction between desiring and intending is most important in the present context because one definition of plans advanced earlier asserted that plans can be thought of as "intentions writ large" (Bratman, 1987). If desire were a species of intention, then desire would be part and parcel of plans themselves, a view that not only conflicts with the present framework, but one that also would call into question the conceptual independence of the desire and plan constructs.

Knowledge and Plan Complexity.   Another important determinant of the complexity of plans is the level of knowledge the planner has about the planning domain under consideration. For instance, individuals pursuing the goal of changing an opinion, who also have large number of facts and arguments germane to the issue, are more likely to be able to develop complex persuasion plans with respect to that issue. However, it might be possible for people to lack knowledge about the specific issue being argued but to have a considerable fund of general knowledge about changing others' opinions. It is thus possible to distinguish between general knowledge that might be used to alter opinions on any issue and knowledge that is specific to the focal issue of a particular persuasion episode. Can this differentiation be generalized to social goals other than opinion change?

Consider the social goal of acquiring personal information from another individual. Berger and Kellermann (1983) and Kellermann and Berger (1984) found that people employed the following three principal means for inducing others to divulge information about themselves: (a) *interrogation*, (b) *disclosing information* about the self to encourage reciprocal disclosure by the other, and (c) *relaxing the target person* to promote self-disclosure. These are abstract categories of strategies that would be similar to such action categories as create arguments or counterargue in the persuasion example. These three information acquisition strategies do not by themselves indicate, respectively, what questions should be asked, what specific information about one's self should be proffered to the other, or what specific behaviors should be enacted to relax the target. However, this example serves to illustrate the general notion that the distinction between general strategic knowledge within a domain and knowledge that is more specific to the local goals being pursued may indeed generalize across social goals.

The distinction between strategic domain knowledge and specific domain knowledge simply reflects the hierarchical nature of plans discussed earlier. In addition to these two types of knowledge is general planning knowledge. Presumably, individuals vary with respect to their ability to engage in planning activities in general, and some individuals are generally more planful than others (Kreitler & Kreitler, 1987). General planning knowledge exerts considerable influence over the ability to develop plans in particular domains. At one extreme, individuals may not be cognizant of the necessity for planning to reach goals, or, somewhat less extreme, people may set goals that they cannot possibly reach, thus rendering their plans useless. At the other extreme, individuals may be acutely aware of the variables that might influence the development of an action plan.

In the interests of both efficiency and the avoidance of disappointment, for example, one would expect general planning knowledge to sensitize planners to the necessity of assessing the potential achievability of goals before expending the effort to plan for their attainment. General planning knowledge should alert planners to be careful to avoid goal and plan conflicts in their own lives, as well as with those with whom they interact. Such general planning knowledge might include the proposition that when planning to reach a social goal of any kind, one should take into account the possible responses by others to one's planned actions, and plan accordingly. At a higher level of abstraction, this proposition might read something like, "it is better to be a sociocentric planner than an egocentric planner when social goals are at stake."

Although the relationship between general planning knowledge and plan complexity is difficult to postulate in any straightforward way, the relationship between strategic domain knowledge, specific domain knowledge, and plan complexity can be summarized in the following proposition:

> Proposition 3: Increases in strategic domain knowledge and specific domain knowledge tend to produce increases in the complexity of plans within that domain.

The distinction between strategic and specific domain knowledge suggests a corollary to Proposition 3. Without considerable strategic domain knowledge, it is difficult to see how one could develop a complex plan. Moreover, a high level of strategic domain knowledge itself may not ensure the development of a complex plan, unless there is a considerable fund of specific domain knowledge with which to flesh out strategic alternatives. This line of argument leads to the interactive relationship posited in Corollary 1:

> Corollary 1: Maximally complex action plans will be generated when high levels of both strategic domain knowledge and specific domain knowledge obtain. Low levels of strategic domain knowledge or high levels of strategic domain knowledge with low levels of specific domain knowledge produce plans with lower levels of complexity.

In the previous section, it was asserted that the strength of the desire to reach a goal determines partially the complexity of the plan devised to reach that goal; however, considering the roles of strategic and specific domain knowledge in the production of plans suggests a modification to the relationship postulated in Proposition 2. Specifically, a situation could be envisioned in which there is a strong desire to reach a particular goal but little knowledge to support the planning effort. Consequently, strong desire, by itself, may not act to promote the generation of complex action plans. The interactive relationship of desire and knowledge on plan complexity is summarized in the following proposition:

> *Proposition 4*: Strength of desire and levels of strategic and specific domain knowledge interact to produce differences in plan complexity. High levels of desire and high levels of knowledge produce more complex plans. Low and high desire levels coupled with low knowledge levels should produce less complex plans.

Meta-Goals and Plan Complexity.   It was suggested previously that the meta-goals of efficiency and social appropriateness are crucial in shaping plans for the attainment of social goals. Wilensky's (1983) approach to planning carries with it the assumption that planning is guided in such a way that the most efficient plan is developed. Whether this is always the case for human planners is an open question; however, it may be that instead of being *optimizers*, human planners are more likely to be *satisficers* (Simon, 1955, 1956). That is, individuals might be prone to develop a plan that they believe will work and that is efficient enough, but one that may not be optimally efficient. Of course, within the context of planning for social goals, it is difficult to assess the notions of efficiency or optimality, at least on a priori grounds. However, when planning for such tasks as running errands (Hayes-Roth, 1980; Hayes-Roth & Hayes-Roth, 1979) or planning the order in which various housekeeping chores might be done in a classroom (Pea & Hawkins, 1987), the concepts of efficiency and optimality are considerably more easily conceptualized and operationalized.

In spite of these problems, it is reasonable to assume that because of cognitive processing limitations and the press of time in everyday social life, there are some pressures toward developing efficient plans to achieve social goals. Moreover, people frequently consider the social appropriateness of their actions as they pursue social goals; although, here again, actions may not necessarily be optimally appropriate. Nonetheless, as pressures toward efficiency and social appropriateness increase, one would expect the complexity with which one plans to be affected systematically. Pressures toward efficiency should direct planners toward more parsimonious plans. Increased emphasis on social appropriateness should restrict the range of alternative actions that the planner might include in the plan. For example, if one's goals are to change another's opinion while at the same time maintaining a close friendship, concerns for social appropriateness of planned actions should restrict the range of alternative actions that might be deployed to attain the opinion-change goal; for example, threatening actions might be excluded.

The idea that the range of actions that might be taken to achieve a goal depends on the degree to which the social actor is sensitive to social appropriateness concerns is reflected in the work done on machiavellianism. Christie and Geis (1970) argued that high Machiavellians are better manipulators than their low Machiavellian counterparts in part because they have neither strong commitments to conventional morality nor high levels of ideological commitment. These two attributes enable high Machiavellians to be more flexible and to adapt their actions to the particular circumstances in which they find themselves. Moreover, their low levels of commitment to conventional morality enable them to consider engaging in unethical actions; thus increasing the breadth of their action repertoires. In support of this relationship, Guterman (1970) found that high Machiavellians reported lower levels of need for approval than did low Machiavellians. Again, not being concerned about approval from others allows high Machiavellians to consider a wider range of actions to achieve their goals. Although the Machiavellian personality is not of central concern in the present context, the theory and research in this area suggest potential empirical support for the following proposition:

Proposition 5: Increased concerns for the meta-goals of efficiency and social appropriateness tend to reduce the complexity of plans to reach social goals.

It should be acknowledged that the meta-goals of efficiency and social appropriateness may either reinforce each other or be in tension with each other. For example, perhaps the most efficient way to acquire personal information from another is to ask personal questions (Berger & Kellermann, 1983, 1989, 1994; Kellermann & Berger, 1984); however, excessive questioning can become intrusive and change an informal social interaction into an interrogation. By contrast, doing all one can to relax another person in order to encourage them to talk about themselves is considerably less intrusive, but may not be particularly efficient; especially if one wishes to obtain specific items of information from the target person. Relaxed targets may reveal considerable information about themselves; however, they may not reveal the desired information. The more intrusive strategy of question-asking increases the likelihood that the desired information will be revealed, but using this strategy may lower social appropriateness. Conversely, when one's social goal is to ingratiate one's self to another, the most efficient way to accomplish this goal also may be the most socially appropriate. Inducing a target individual to like one by smiling and being friendly is likely to give rise to elevated social appropriateness judgments.

It is difficult to make any general statement concerning the relationship between the metagoals of efficiency and social appropriateness. As is evident from the previous discussion, they can either complement each other or be in tension with each other; in either case, however, each goal appears to exert a similar effect on the complexity with which plans are developed.

From Plans to Social Actions: The Hierarchy Principle

Thwarted Goals and Iterative Planning.   People may enter interactions with well-thought-out plans for achieving goals only to find that, for a variety of reasons, the path to their goal or goals is blocked. Although blocked progress toward goals is a potential source of frustration to planners, it is also true that more is learned about individuals' planning capabilities when their path to a goal is blocked. Immediate success in reaching goals obviates the necessity of assessing alternative plans that individuals may or may not possess; moreover, it is when goal failure occurs that people are forced to devise alternative plans, which, in turn, may require learning (Schank, 1982, 1986). Thwarted progress toward goals affords the opportunity to study individuals' planning capabilities.

In social interaction contexts, there are two principal sources of goal blockage. First, events that are *external* to the interaction may interfere with goal attainment. For example, a suitor who plans to ask a woman to marry him when they are alone may be thwarted by the unanticipated presence of other persons in the immediate situation; or people who are discussing a third party may be prevented from pursuing the discussion further when the third party appears. A second source of blockage is *internal* to the interaction itself. Co-interactants may resist each other's attempts to change their opinions, or interactants may repel ingratiation attempts. As was pointed out previously, both external and internal sources of thwarting may be anticipated by the planner and accounted for in the development of contingency plans. The main concern in the present discussion is with internal sources, and it is assumed that strength of desire is sufficient so that thwarting does not induce goal abandonment.

The Hierarchy Principle.   Given the hierarchical organization of plans, an important question concerns what happens to action choices when plans are thwarted. For instance, assume that an individual attempts to persuade another to change an opinion by using a particular argument. Further, suppose that the other resists the opinion change attempt. Finally, assume that the persuader's plan has alternative actions for achieving the goal, and that these actions are represented at different levels of abstraction in the hierarchy. This scenario contains several possibilities for the thwarted planner. First, the planner may continue to repeat the same argument, perhaps increasing vocal intensity or varying some other aspect of paralanguage at the same time (Ringle & Bruce, 1980). Such paralinguistic alterations would constitute very low-level changes in the plan hierarchy. Second, the planner might invoke another specific argument, thus altering the plan at a somewhat more abstract level of the hierarchy. Finally, the planner could modify even more abstract plan elements and the order in which these plan units are enacted. For example, rather than taking the offensive by deploying arguments, the planner might challenge the target to advance arguments for their position, thus raising the possibility that the planner could refute these arguments. In terms of the terminology introduced earlier, the difference between the second and third options involves the difference between a change in specific domain knowledge—invoking a new argument—and a change in strategic domain knowledge—instantiating a new abstract plan unit, refuting opposing arguments.

The difficulty with accomplishing alterations to plans that involve highly abstract plan units is that changes in these units imply plan alterations that cascade down the hierarchy and require that less abstract plan units also be altered. Moreover, alterations to the sequencing of abstract units imply similar processing demands. These plan alteration strategies fly in the face of the two postulates discussed in connection with the explication of Proposition 1, namely: (a) individuals have limited information-processing resources with which to make alterations to plans (Hogarth, 1980; Kahneman, Slovic, & Tversky, 1982; Kunda & Nisbett, 1986; Nisbett & Ross, 1980), and (b) people are wont to expend these limited resources (Fiske & Taylor, 1984, 1991). Consequently, the confluence of these postulates suggests the following proposition:

> Proposition 6: When people experience thwarting internal to the interaction, their first response is likely to involve low-level plan hierarchy alterations. Continued thwarting will tend to produce more abstract alterations to plan hierarchies.

This proposition suggests that when goal blocks occur, social interactants will repeat the previous action sequence with minor, low-level variations. Of course, given memory limitations, individuals cannot literally replicate what they have said and done previously, even after very short time intervals between repetitions.

The following corollary to Proposition 6 can be drawn from the previous discussion of goal desire. Individuals who have elevated goal desire levels should be willing to expend more time and effort to alter plans at more abstract levels when their plans are thwarted:

> Corollary 1: Elevated levels of goal desire will propel planners to make more abstract alterations to plan hierarchies when their plans to reach social goals fail.

In addition, given repeated goal failures, higher levels of goal desire should induce planners to make higher level changes earlier in the goal failure–plan alteration sequence. Stated formally:

> Corollary 2: Planners with high levels of goal desire, who experience repeated thwarting of goal-directed actions, will manifest higher level alterations to their plans earlier in the goal failure–plan alteration sequence than will planners with lower levels of goal desire who experience repeated goal failure.

Proposition 6 and its two corollaries make up the current incarnation of the *Hierarchy Principle*. A detailed discussion of the research evidence bearing on this principle is presented in chapter 4.

Goal Failure and Affect.   Not only does goal thwarting have the cognitive and action consequences just spelled out in the Hierarchy Principle, it has affective consequences as well. It has been suggested that unpredictable events give rise to autonomic nervous system (ANS) arousal that, in turn, is experienced as emotion (Berscheid, 1983; Mandler, 1975; Sternberg, 1986). The consequences of this arousal can be considerable. For example, a number of theorists concur that it is the unpredictability involved in early stages of romantic relationships that fuels the strong emotions that characterize feelings of romantic love (Berscheid, 1983; Livingston, 1980; Sternberg, 1986). As relationships age and individuals become more predictable, the extreme levels of emotions experienced by relationship partners tend to dampen down.

Srull and Wyer (1986) extended this line of argument to the domain of goal-directed action. They asserted that when a goal is attained, positive affect tends to be generated. By contrast, when planned actions are thwarted, people are likely to experience negative affect. In addition to these gross predictions, they specified the conditions that are likely to affect the magnitude of negative affect felt when progress toward a goal is interrupted. First, the more important the goal being pursued, the greater the intensity of the negative affect displayed. The second factor involved is the psychological distance from the superordinate goal at which the interruption occurs. The closer individuals feel they are to the superordinate goal, the more intense the negative affect when an interruption takes place. Of course, if there are contingency plans available that enable the planner to circumvent the interruption, then the intensity of the negative affect generated should be reduced. Finally, the level of *investment* of time and energy toward reaching the goal is a third determinant. High investment levels tend to produce more intense negative affect when failure occurs.

Although the relationships posited by Srull and Wyer (1986) seem to be intuitively plausible, there are some potential exceptions to them. Consider first the situation in which a goal is achieved, one that would seem almost always to produce positive affect, according to Srull and Wyer (1986). There are instances in which people have achieved highly sought-after superordinate goals only to be disappointed once they have achieved them. Sudden increases in wealth may not result in concomitant increases in felt happiness; or obtaining a highly desired job may turn out not to be as fulfilling as it was expected to be. One might object to these examples on the grounds that, in these cases, the negative affect is generated some time after the goal itself is attained. The initial response to achieving the goal—for example, winning the lottery or landing the desired job—might be quite positive. It is only after passage of some time and some reflection that the positive affect turns negative; however, these examples may not be as compelling as they seem. Some people who win lotteries may think of the potential complications to their lives that such large sums of money might bring, including the potential hordes of people seeking to sell them various products and services. These realizations could occur even before the winners have learned of their good fortune.

The other question is whether interruptions in plans are necessarily likely to produce negative affect, even when the goal is important, the interruption takes place close to the goal, and the amount of investment is high. Consider the case of individuals who report that events that interfered with their attaining a particular goal actually prevented them from making a terrible mistake; the interruption prevented them from achieving a goal they really did not want to attain. In such cases, interruptions may produce positive affect. Again, this possibility might be objected to on the grounds that this kind of evaluation represents rationalization and is likely to occur sometime after the interruption has taken place. Thus, this counterargument would suggest that in such situations, individuals initially respond negatively to goal failure and subsequently rationalize their failures. One possible rejoinder to this counterargument would be that because individuals can evaluate the desirability of goals as they progress toward them, it is possible that people might continue to follow plans toward goals only to welcome an interruption because the desirability of the goal has decreased over time. In this case, an interruption might not simply produce less negative affect because of the decrease in the desirability of the goal; it might produce relief and positive affect because the individual can stop "going through the motions."

The issue raised here revolves around the notion of *superordinate goal* as used by Srull and Wyer (1986). In a particular context, one might be able to identify a superordinate goal or goals toward which individuals are striving; however, such context-specific goals are embedded in still broader contexts, and in these broader contexts the context-specific superordinate goal may be a subordinate goal to an extra-context-specific goal or goals. The problem is that when people formulate and plan to attain context-specific goals, they may not think of how these goals fit with extra-context, superordinate goals. For example, assume that an individual has the goal of leading a happy life. This broad life goal lurks in the background, but rarely does the person think of how to achieve it directly. Assume that the same person has the more specific goal of winning a lot of money in the lottery. Suppose the person wins the lottery. It does not seem farfetched to suppose that the person may suddenly realize that the goal of having a lot of money is incompatible with the broader life goal of being happy. Furthermore, not winning the lottery may make the person happy, if the relationships between the broad life goal and implications of winning the lottery become salient.

The general scenario implied by this example is hardly a rare one in everyday life. Individuals who spend considerable time and effort obtaining degrees in law and medicine sometimes come to realize that a career in these areas is not compatible with their broader life goals. As a result, they seek other, potentially more fulfilling careers.

Assuming that context-specific superordinate goals are compatible with broader, extra-context goals, the following proposition can be advanced:

Proposition 7: Attainment of a superordinate goal will produce positive affect. Interruption of a plan will result in the induction of negative affect.

Given Srull and Wyer's (1986) conditions and the points made in the previous discussion, the following corollaries to Proposition 7 can be generated:

Corollary 1: The intensity of affect experienced after goal attainment or interruption is positively related to the importance of the goal.

Corollary 2: Given the unavailability of contingency plans, the closer to the goal the interruption occurs, the more intense the negative affect will be. The presence of contingency plans will tend to dampen the intensity of negative affect experienced.

Corollary 3: The greater the investment of time and energy in the pursuit of a goal, the more intense the negative affect experienced will be when interruption occurs. Again, the presence of contingency plans will tend to dampen the intensity of negative affect.

The fact that thwarting plans at a specific point can give rise to negative affect raises the issue of what happens both to affect and planning when repeated goal failure occurs. Here it is assumed that the desire to attain the goal is of sufficient strength that the social actor continues to pursue the goal, even after several unsuccessful attempts. Generally, one would suppose that out of ordinary concerns for social approval, individuals would attempt to maximize the likelihood of goal attainment by developing or instantiating the most socially appropriate course of action and holding in abeyance potentially less socially appropriate, although perhaps more efficient, alternative plans. Failure of more socially appropriate courses of action should lead, by default, to the development of increasingly less socially appropriate plans. This relationship is represented in the following proposition:

Proposition 8: Repeated thwarting of plans will lead to the instantiation and enactment of progressively less socially appropriate plans.

Of course, the lengths to which one might go to achieve a particular goal may depend on how important the goal is. This possibility suggests the following corollary to Proposition 8:

Corollary 1: The importance of the goal determines the extent to which one will continue to deploy successively less socially appropriate plans in response to thwarting. The more important to goal, the more one will be willing to employ less socially appropriate plans.

The social appropriateness metagoal will set the lower bound past which individuals will not go in pursuing a social goal. Once this lower bound is reached—assuming that the individual still desires to reach the goal—the person may be forced to reiterate previous plans that fall within the permissible range of social appropriateness.

It is also important to recognize that negative affect induced by repeated thwarting may have impacts on the planning process itself; that is, it is assumed that there is a feedback loop from the affective state to the working memory where planning takes place. As negative affect increases with repeated goal failure, one would expect the capacity of working memory to be adversely affected such that the ability to devise complex plans decreases. This relationship is summarized in the following proposition:

Proposition 9: With repeated thwarting over time, resulting in the induction of higher levels of negative affect, plans will become progressively less complex.

Proposition 5 suggested that relaxing the influence of the social appropriateness metagoal allows for the creation of more planning options, thus increasing the complexity of plans. This proposition could be read as conflicting with the relationships posited in Proposition 9; however, this is not the case. The relationships advanced in Proposition 5 did not take into account the potential affect generated during the interaction itself. All other things being equal, lowering concerns for social appropriateness should increase the breadth of plan options, as indicated in Proposition 5. As the interaction progresses, however, and socially appropriate options are exhausted *and* the intensity of negative affect increases because of continued thwarting, the complexity of the plan remaining to be enacted is affected adversely by the elevated intensity of negative affect.

Plan Complexity and Action Fluidity.   In the previous section, the cognitive and affective consequences of goal failure were discussed. Here we consider how the complexity of plans influences the fluidity with which they are enacted. The term *fluidity* is used here to encompass both verbal and nonverbal aspects of plan performance. Although the term *verbal fluency* appears regularly in the communication literature, its logical counterpart *nonverbal fluency* is virtually never used. Nevertheless, such nonverbal parameters as self- and object-focused adaptors and the fluidity with which gesticulation is enacted might be empirical indicators of the nonverbal fluency construct. The term *action fluidity* is used here to refer to the verbal and nonverbal fluency with which a plan is enacted. The action fluidity construct is not necessarily directly related to the ultimate effectiveness with which a plan is enacted, although it might be related indirectly. The ultimate effectiveness of a plan obviously depends on the content of the plan as well as they way in which the plan is enacted. Nevertheless, there is considerable evidence supporting the assertion that verbally fluent individuals are judged to be more credible and influential than their less fluent counterparts (Berger, 1994). Consequently, although the content of the plan will be a very direct determinant of its effectiveness, the fluidity with which it is enacted will have at least an indirect influence. The issue of plan effectiveness is considered in greater detail in chapter 5 of this volume.

It might be argued that individuals who can instantiate or devise plans that contain numerous alternative paths for reaching a goal are likely to manifest fluid performances of their plans. This might especially be the case when plans are thwarted; that is, in the extreme case, when an individual has only one way of attaining a goal and that path is blocked, that individual has no alternative course of action to which to turn. Of course, in response to thwarting, the individual could either abandon the goal or reiterate the course of action. By contrast, the person with a complex plan, consisting of a number of contingency subplans, presumably would find responding to continued thwarting considerably easier. Although this line of reasoning has potential merit, there are some difficulties with it. For example, at any given point in a plan, as the number of available courses of action increases past just a few, the planner is presented with an increasingly complex decision-making task if alternative courses of action must be chosen. The plan with only a few alternative courses of action from which to choose presents a decision-making environment with less uncertainty. Consequently, it is the planner with fewer alternatives available who will be faced with lower uncertainty levels and thus manifest a more fluid performance.

A synthesis of these two positions is rendered possible by advancing the following proposition:

> *Proposition 10:* Under conditions of goal failure, individuals whose plans contain no alternative actions and those whose plans contain numerous action alternatives at the point of thwarting will manifest lower levels of action fluidity than those whose plans contain a small number of contingent actions.

This curvilinear proposition is premised on the idea that plan complexity as indexed by the number of contingent actions present in the plan is not a general trait; that is, the complexity of plans is specific to a particular planning domain. Thus, one would not expect plan complexity in one goal domain to predict action fluidity in another goal domain, and one also would not expect very high correlations between complexity levels among domains.

Access to Plans and Action Fluidity. Although plans may be instantiated from a long-term store or generated in a working memory, there may be differential access to planned actions; that is, planned actions may be differentially retrievable. It is not enough to have planned certain actions; these conceptual representations of actions must be available and accessible when they are needed. If they are not, action fluidity necessarily will decrease. Moreover, under conditions of thwarting, access to action alternatives must be high to maintain action fluidity. Increased access to a complex plan, however, could adversely affect action fluidity because of the uncertainty problem discussed previously; the presence of many action alternatives could reduce fluidity. Increased access to planned actions in general should increase the fluidity with which action is performed, but it might serve to amplify the curvilinear relationship between the number of action alternatives and action fluidity advanced in Proposition 10. This possibility is expressed in the following proposition:

Proposition 11: Increased access to planned actions will generally increase action fluidity levels in such a way that the curvilinear relationship between the number of alternatives and action fluidity will be maintained but displaced upward relative to the same function obtained under conditions of reduced action access.

SUMMARY

In this chapter the concepts of plan and planning were explicated and embedded in a series of theoretical propositions. The effects of goal desire, general knowledge and domain specific knowledge, and the efficiency and appropriateness of metagoals on plan complexity were outlined. The consequences of goal failure on both subsequent planning and action production were also considered. In addition, the effects of both goal attainment and goal failure on affect were addressed. In the chapters that follow, research bearing on the viability of several of these propositions is presented.

Chapter 3

Plan Complexity

ဢ ◆ ဢ

This chapter addresses two broad questions with respect to plan complexity. First, what antecedent conditions promote variations in the complexity with which plans are formulated? Second, what are the consequences of variations in plan complexity on communicative performance? The first of these two questions embodies the relationships posited in Propositions 2–5. The second question is particularly relevant to Propositions 10 and 11. Not all of the propositions and corollaries advanced in the previous chapter have been tested directly; those that have are the focus of the present and subsequent chapters. The evidence at hand may at times allow for some informed speculation about the viability of yet-to-be-tested propositions.

A word of caution is in order regarding the potential relationships between plan complexity and communicative performance. It is tempting to assume that those with more complex plans will somehow perform better in most communication situations. Depending on what one means by the notion of "performing better," the action fluidity propositions (Propositions 10–11) presented in the last chapter suggest that plan complexity is not an unmixed blessing in guiding communicative performance. In short, more complexity is not necessarily better; although, at times, situational contingencies may demand high levels of plan complexity. Evidence concerning the potentially debilitating effects of plan complexity on communicative performance are considered in the later sections of this chapter.

PRECURSORS OF PLAN COMPLEXITY

There are at least two broad classes of variables that could impact on plan complexity. The first of these, individual difference variables, are enduring but not immutable tendencies people bring with them to planning situations. The second set of relevant factors is active in the planning environment itself, and produces variations in the complexity with which individuals plan. It is difficult to stipulate a priori which of these two sets of

42

variables is prepotent with respect to how they influence the complexity of plans produced in a given social context. Most probably, environmental cues act to elevate or lower the relative contribution of these variable sets to plan complexity. No attempt is made here to explicate these cues and the manner in which they affect the relative salience of individual differences and situational factors, but throughout the following discussion, this problem needs to be heeded.

Individual Differences

Planning Efficacy Beliefs.   One of the most fundamental determinants of plan complexity is the degree to which individuals believe that planning is a useful activity to pursue in any situation. Those who believe that it is better to be "spontaneous" when pursuing goals than to engage in planning before trying to attain goals should be less likely to have well-articulated plans. However, given the orientation of the present framework, if the actions of those who claim to be acting "spontaneously" can be identified as "goal-directed," then it can be assumed that a plan, perhaps one that is not consciously available to the "spontaneous" actors, is guiding their conduct. This view, then, allows for the possibility of planned spontaneity.

The influence of beliefs about the efficacy of planning on plan complexity has been studied directly by Kreitler and Kreitler (1987). These researchers assessed children's (ages 5, 7, 9, and 11 years) general beliefs about the efficacy of planning by asking them a series of questions that allowed the children to indicate the degree to which they felt that planning was a desirable or undesirable activity. The children were presented with a number of different activities (e.g., playing a game and spending a night with a friend or relative), and asked to indicate for each one the extent to which they felt that it would be desirable to prepare for the activity before engaging in it. Responses to these scenarios were aggregated and a total score for each child was computed.

In what was ostensibly a separate study, children who had completed the measure just described were asked to devise plans for reaching a variety of goals. Their plans were then analyzed along a large number of different dimensions, including the number of alternative plans presented, the number of if–then eventualities considered in the plans (contingencies), the number of steps in the plan, and number of alternative steps. Comparisons of the plans devised by children whose general beliefs supported the desirability of planning, with plans developed by children whose beliefs did not, revealed that children who believed in the efficacy of planning generally produced more elaborate and complex plans along these dimensions than their more spontaneous counterparts. An important age trend observed in the data involved the magnitude of the plan complexity differences among children with different planning orientations. Among the five-year-old children, the relationships between planning orientation and the plan complexity measures were all in the predicted direction, but several were not statistically significant. However, as age increased, from 7 through 11 years, the magnitudes of the differences on the plan complexity measures increased as a function of planning orientation.

The results of this study provide strong support for the notion that individuals who hold general beliefs that support the efficacy of planning are more likely to develop more complex plans when asked to engage in planning activity. Moreover, the study suggests that children as young as age five have already begun to develop differential orientations toward the desirability of engaging in planful activity, and these differential orientations have an impact on the degree to which children of this age devise complex plans. In addition, as children grow older, the differential planning orientations exert progressively greater influence on plan complexity. Unfortunately, this study did not take the next step to see whether and how the differences in plan complexity would be reflected in actions directed toward the achievement of the goal for which the plan had been generated. Consequently, we do not know the degree to which differential commitment to planning as an activity is reflected in goal-directed activity, as potentially mediated by level of plan complexity.

Self-Monitoring.   Snyder (1974, 1987) argued that during their interactions with others, individuals can base their actions primarily on their inferences about what will please their interaction partners. Individuals may also predicate their actions on their beliefs of how they should act, regardless of whether these actions will make them attractive to their partners. Snyder labeled individuals who adjust their actions in accordance with their partner's preferences "high self-monitors," whereas those who "say it the way they feel it," Snyder dubbed "low self-monitors." Given these differences in interaction style, high self-monitors would be expected to be more attentive to others and to gather more information about them in order to be able to ingratiate themselves. Indeed, evidence suggests that high self-monitors gather both more information and more diagnostic information about others with whom they anticipate interaction than do their low self-monitoring counterparts (Berger & Douglas, 1981; Berscheid, Graziano, Monson, & Dermer, 1976; Elliot, 1979).

Given the proclivity for high self-monitors to acquire more information about social interaction partners, this increased information intake should result in more complex plans. This hypothesis was tested directly in a study in which individuals were asked to devise negotiation plans before engaging in a bargaining task (Jordan & Roloff, 1995). Several different bargaining tactics were identified by analyzing the plan protocols. The number of tactics included in each planner's protocol was computed to index the diversity of strategies contained in the plan. This diversity measure was then correlated with the self-presentation subscale of the Revised Self-Monitoring Scale (Lennox & Wolfe, 1984). The correlation between this self-monitoring subscale and the diversity measure was significant ($r = .27$, $p < .02$). Consistent with the previous reasoning, high self-monitors devised more complex negotiation plans than did low self-monitors.

Cognitive Complexity.   Extending Kelly's (1955) theory of personal constructs, constructivist researchers examined the relationships between the complexity with which individuals construe others and a host of consequent variables. The number of constructs people employ in their thinking about others partially determines their level of cognitive complexity. The greater the number of unique constructs, the greater the cognitive differentiation or complexity. The literature concerning cognitive complexity is too voluminous to review here; however, a number of extensive reviews of this literature are available (Applegate, 1990; Burleson, 1987, 1989).

Because it has been found that individuals scoring high in cognitive complexity tend to form more elaborate impressions of others after interacting with them (Hale & Delia, 1976), one might reason that the plans generated by cognitively complex individuals should be more complex than those of their less complex counterparts. This should be the case because highly complex individuals should take into account more potential alternative responses in their planning because of their more differentiated perceptions of others.

Waldron and Applegate (1994) asked research participants to complete a cognitive complexity measure, and at a later date engage in a conversation about an issue over which they disagreed. After completing their interactions, research participants individually reviewed a videotape of their interaction and were asked to indicate what actions they were planning to take and what actions they decided against taking during each 60-second interval of the taped conversation. The responses to these questions were used to construct measures of plan complexity, plan sophistication, plan specificity, and editing. The degree to which individuals employed competent verbal disagreement tactics was also coded from the taped conversations.

The cognitive complexity measure along with the plan and editing measures were regressed against the degree of competence manifested in the disagreement tactics employed by those involved in the interactions. These analyses showed that cognitive complexity accounted for virtually no variance in the competence measure; however, when the plan and editing measures were included in the equation, the amount of variance accounted for in competence increased by 14%.

Although these findings suggest that planning and editing processes employed during disagreement situations are more important determinants of the degree to which competent disagreement tactics are used than is the degree to which individual interactants are cognitively complex, other evidence suggested that cognitive complexity may be a useful predictor of the degree to which plans are complex, specific, and sophisticated, and the degree to which planned actions are edited. Correlations between cognitive complexity and these measures were all statistically significant and ranged from .21 to .49, indicating that individuals with high levels of cognitive complexity tend to develop plans that are more complex, specific, and sophisticated than their less complex counterparts. Moreover, highly complex individuals also tended to engage in more editing of their planned actions. However, the fact that the three plan variables themselves were intercorrelated substantially with each other (r's ranged from .78 to .87) raises some questions about the independence of these three plan constructs. Nevertheless, these findings indicate that although cognitive complexity is not a particularly good predictor of interaction behavior (Denton, Sprenkle, & Burleson, 1993), it seems to account for some variance in the characteristics of plans that individuals produce and the editing processes they employ while enacting them.

Comment. Given that measures of planning efficacy beliefs, self-monitoring, and cognitive complexity all have been found to account for some variance in plan complexity measures, it is important that future research go beyond the intrinsic limitations of the zero order correlation and employ multivariate techniques to determine the degree to which these individual difference measures themselves are intercorrelated, and to what extent they account for unique portions of variance in plan complexity indices. As theoretically and practically interesting as zero order correlations between individual difference measures and plan complexity indexes might be, a complete picture of the role of individual differences in promoting the development of complex plans will not be understood if these relationships continue to be studied piecemeal.

Situational Influences

Although it is evident that potentially enduring individual differences have an impact on the propensity both to engage in planning and to plan in more or less detail once committed to planful activity, there are a host of situationally based factors that could influence the degree to which individuals generate complex plans. Such obvious candidates as goal desire (Propositions 2 & 4), the amount of time available for planning (Berger, 1985), and the degree to which the planner is uncertain about the ultimate attainability of goals (Berger, 1995b) should exert direct and powerful effects on the degree to which plans are complex. Although data bearing directly on all but one of these obvious candidates are presently lacking, there are other, somewhat less obvious situational factors that might exert direct influences on the degree to which complex plans are generated. Two of these variables are considered here after data germane to the goal desire–plan complexity relationship are reviewed.

Goal Desire and Plan Complexity.   There is some indirect evidence to support the idea, expressed in Proposition 2, that increases in goal desire are likely to be associated with increases in plan complexity (Berger, 1988c). As part of a larger study, individuals were asked to write plans to persuade another person to adopt their position on two different attitude issues. Before writing their plans, participants indicated their positions on each of the two issues using five-point Likert scales. The number of action units in each of the persuasion plans was determined for each participant to provide an estimate of plan complexity. In addition, the degree to which each individual's opinion deviated from neutral for each of the two issues was computed as an index of issue involvement such that the greater the deviation, the greater the involvement.

Across both attitude issues combined, the correlation between issue involvement and the number of action units in the plan was .40 ($p < .001$), indicating that those with higher levels of issue involvement tended to produce more complex plans. Although opinion polarization is probably not a precise indicator of issue involvement, and issue involvement, in turn, is not a precise measure of goal desire (although one would expect those who are more involved with an issue to be more active persuaders if given the opportunity), it is close enough to such a measure that the positive correlation between it and plan complexity can be taken as indirect support for Proposition 2. Of course, replicating the relationship between plan complexity and goal desire using more direct empirical indicators of goal desire would help provide the measurement triangulation necessary to increase confidence in the viability of Proposition 2.

Interrogating Extant Plans.   As was argued in Proposition 1, when individuals desire to achieve goals, they first attempt to retrieve an extant plan from memory to guide their actions. However, these canned plans most likely will require some measure of modification because, in principle, they cannot match exactly any previous circumstances in which they were used, because no two situations, no matter how similar they may appear to be, are exactly alike. If extant plans are questioned with respect to what planners would do in the event that specific actions contained in them were to fail, planners should respond by generating contingent actions to anticipate such sources of goal blockage. By generating such contingent actions, their plans should become more complex.

This hypothesis was tested directly in an experiment in which individuals were asked to write plans for persuading another person to adopt their position on an attitudinal issue (Berger, Karol, & Jordan, 1989, Experiment

3). Half of those who generated these persuasion plans were provided a copy of their plan and asked what they would do in the event that four randomly selected actions in their plan failed to bring about the desired result. Thus, for example, if the randomly selected action was an argument, participants were asked what they would do next if they used the argument and it failed to persuade the other person. Or, if the randomly selected action had to do with a tactical maneuver, such as asking the target why they held their opinion, the participant was asked what would be done next if, after deploying that tactic, it failed to bring about the desired end-state. During the same interval, the other participants in this experiment were asked to indicate the outstanding characteristics of four different political candidates. After completing these tasks, all participants were asked to write another persuasion plan for the same opinion topic as the first persuasion plan.

Comparison of the pre- and post-interrogation plans showed that the post-interrogation plans of those who were questioned directly about their plans contained significantly more new arguments than did the plans of those who were not questioned about their plans. New arguments were those that appeared in the post-interrogation plans that were not part of the preinterrogation plans. Consequently, the process of questioning plans had the effect of inducing planners to think of alternative arguments they had not considered before and to include these new arguments in the second rendition of their plans.

Although this finding provides general support for the notion that questioning plans before their deployment is likely to increase their complexity, there is at least one potential limitation to this relationship not made explicit in this experiment. One presupposition underlying this relationship is that when individuals are asked what they would do in the event an action failed to bring about a desired goal state, the individuals so interrogated have available to them in memory some alternatives that might be used to overcome the imagined barrier. It seems possible that under some circumstances, individuals might not be able to generate any alternatives in response to such questioning. For such planners, it would not be reasonable to expect increments in the number of unique actions contained in subsequent plans. Although this kind of extreme case was not generally encountered in the experiment just described, it remains a theoretical possibility.

Priming Planning Activity.   Interrogating individuals about their planned actions in the manner just described represents a very direct, blunderbuss-like approach to provoking the development of more complex plans. A somewhat more indirect and subtle way to reach the same goal would be to place planners in a situation in which they engage in a task not directly concerned with developing the plan itself, but one that is germane to the development of the plan. As was noted in Proposition 3 and the discussion surrounding it in chapter 2, as individuals acquire specific knowledge about others, they can incorporate that knowledge into their plans such that when they wish to achieve a goal involving the specific others, they can tailor their plans accordingly. By sensitizing planners to the possible unique characteristics of target individuals and the specific attributes of the situation in which the plan is likely to be carried out before they actually develop a plan to achieve a goal, planners, so sensitized, should devise more complex plans than planners for whom such considerations are not made salient.

Note that in the formulation of this particular hypothesis, it is not necessary that the planner actually receive information germane to the target individual or to the situation in which the plan will be enacted for plan complexity to increase; although, consistent with Proposition 3, increased knowledge should promote increased plan complexity. Simply inducing the planner to think about these possibilities should be sufficient to encourage the generation of plans with greater complexity. In addition, the degree to which planners think along multiple, unique dimensions of person and situation information should be related to the complexity with which they plan. Specifically, the more dimensions along which they think, the greater the complexity. Again, these effects should be evident in plans even though planners do not actually receive information relevant to these dimensions.

These hypotheses were tested directly in an experiment in which individuals were asked to devise plans for reaching two different social goals (Berger & diBattista, 1992a). Experimental participants were randomly assigned to develop and plan for one of the two following goals: (a) asking someone out for a date (Date Request), and (b) inducing a new roommate to like one (Roommate Ingratiation). In addition, within each one of these goal conditions, individuals were randomly assigned to two conditions. In the Before condition, participants were informed that they would be devising a plan to reach one of the two goals, but before devising their plan, they were asked to list the kinds of information they would like to have about the person toward whom they would be directing their actions and the situation within which they would be interacting with that person, in order for them to develop a more effective plan. By contrast, in the After condition, participants first devised plans for their assigned goals and then were asked to list the personal and situational information they would like to have to develop a better plan, as those in the Before condition had been instructed.

Given the theoretical framework of this study, requesting person and situation information in advance of planning, as those in the Before condition did, should sensitize these planners in such a way that their plans should be more complex than those in the After condition, who were sensitized to person and situation variables after they already had committed themselves to a specific plan. For those in the After condition, then, the planning horse was already out of the cognitive barn. Moreover, among those in the Before condition, those requesting more unique items of personal and situational information should devise more complex plans than those requesting fewer pieces of such information because unique items of information represent attributes of persons and situations. It is important to keep in mind here that the diversity of the information sought could be more important than the sheer number of items of information requested. For example, asking for large a number of items of information from the same category (e.g. biographical information), might not promote as much plan complexity as asking for the same number of items of information distributed over a diverse set of information categories, (e.g. biographical, personality, attitudes, preferences, etc.). Given this reasoning, information diversity should be a better predictor of plan complexity than the sheer number of items of information requested, because the gross number of items generated might contain some measure of redundancy. In this study, plan complexity was determined by counting the number of conceptual action units (CAU's) contained in participants' plans. In addition, the number of contingencies included in each plan was determined.

The results of this study generally supported the hypotheses. First, for those in the Date Request condition, participants who sought personal and situational information before they wrote their plans (Before condition) included significantly more CAU units in their plans than did those who sought the personal and situational information after they wrote their plans (After condition); however, this predicted difference was not significant for those who wrote plans in the Roommate Ingratiation condition. The plans of those in the Date Request condition contained significantly more contingencies than those who wrote plans in the Roommate Ingratiation condition.

The difficulty with the foregoing analyses is that they ignore the amount and diversity of personal and situational information sought by study participants. To rectify this shortcoming, within-condition correlations were computed between the quantity and diversity of person and situation information sought on the one hand, and the number of CAU's and contingencies included in the plans on the other. These correlations are shown in Table 3.1.

As the data displayed in Table 3.1 clearly indicate, the information quantity and diversity measures correlated significantly with the number of CAU's appearing in plans only when personal and situational information was sought before the plans were written. When information was sought after the plans had been written, the correlations were all nonsignificant. Although the differences between the Before and After condition correlations between information quantity and CAU's generated in each of the two

TABLE 3.1

Within Condition Correlations Between Information Seeking
and Plan Complexity Measures

Condition	Information Quantity With		Information Diversity With	
	CAU's	Contingencies	CAU's	Contingencies
Date-Request-Before	.48*	−.11	.62**	.09
Date-Request-After	.34	.29	.17	.03
Roommate-Before	.64**	.17	.77***	.43*
Roomate-After	.31	−.01	.24	.02

*p < .05; **p < .01; *** p < .001. Table adapted from Berger and DiBattista (1992a). Reprinted with permission from the Speech Communication Association.

goal conditions were not significant, the same comparisons of the correlations between information diversity and number of CAU's included in plans were significantly different. This result comports with the hypothesis advanced earlier that the diversity of person and situation information sought is a better predictor of plan complexity than the gross amount of information sought before planning.

Table 3.1 shows that the quantity of information sought was not significantly related to the number of contingencies included in plans in any of the experimental conditions. Although this was generally true for the information diversity measure, those who requested information across more categories in the Roommate–Before condition tended to include more contingencies in their plans than those who requested information from a less diverse set of categories. In general, individuals did not include numerous contingencies in their plans (Date Request, M = 1.35; Roommate Ingratiation, M = .50); consequently, the general lack of variability in the contingency measures may have suppressed potential relationships between these measures and the information-seeking measures.

Although the results of this study lend support to the theoretical notion advanced earlier that individuals who are encouraged to seek diverse pieces of information about the person and situation within which a given plan will be executed are more likely to develop more elaborate plans in terms of their overall length, a serendipitous finding of this study concerns the significant differences in the number of plan contingencies observed between the Date Request and Roommate Ingratiation conditions. Why might individuals be more prone to include contingencies in date-request plans than in their plans for ingratiating themselves to a roommate? One potential answer to this question concerns the differential amount of face loss that one might experience between these two goals in the event of goal failure. For most individuals, asking for a date and being turned down most probably potentiates considerably more embarrassment than attempting to induce a new roommate to like one and then failing to do so. Consequently, in planning for the date-request goal, individuals might be more prone to think of potential points of failure in the plan and spontaneously develop contingencies to deal with them than when planning for the roommate-ingratiation goal. If this line of reasoning has merit, as potential face loss increases, so should the tendency to include contingencies in plans. Of course, this hypothesis could and should be evaluated in a study in which the potential face loss involved in goal failure is determined for a variety of goals, and the degree to which contingencies are included in plans for attaining these goals is assessed.

ACTION CONSEQUENCES OF PLAN COMPLEXITY

As noted in the previous discussion, studies linking individual difference variables to plan complexity typically have not gone on to study the next link in the theoretical chain, namely the relationship between plan complexity and the production of social action. In the present context, these relationships are embodied in theoretical Propositions 10 and 11. Proposition 10 asserted that under conditions of plan failure, when social interactants who wish to continue to pursue their goals are forced to choose alternative courses of action, individuals with no alternatives or those with numerous alternatives will demonstrate lower levels of action fluidity than individuals with moderate numbers of alternatives. It is not possible to stipulate the inflection points of this curvilinear relationship between plan complexity and action fluidity so that a precise prediction might be made with respect to the number of alternatives that would constitute too many options. Proposition 11 argued that variations in access to action representations would affect the location of the curve described in Proposition 10 such that increased access to planned actions would tend to displace the function upward. That is, the curve would maintain its shape but move upward as a function of increased access to action representations.

Plan Complexity and Action Fluidity

When a Lot of Knowledge is a Dangerous Thing.   An experiment dealing directly with Proposition 10 was reported by Berger, Karol, and Jordan (1989, Experiment 1). The overall structure of this experiment required all participants to present arguments supporting their position on a current campus issue to another student who, unbeknownst to the participants, was an experimental confederate. These confederates were instructed both to allow the participants to present their arguments and not to respond either positively or negatively to the initial argument. However, as the interaction proceeded, confederates showed progressively more disagreement with participants' arguments. These interactions were videotaped for further analysis.

Before engaging in the persuasion task, participants were randomly divided into three experimental conditions. Those in the No Plan condition were simply given the topic on which they were to present their arguments and, with no opportunity for advanced preparation, they completed the persuasion task. Individuals in the Plan Only condition were asked to write a plan for persuading another student on the experimental issue before performing the persuasion task. As soon as they completed the plan, they were taken to another room where they engaged in the persuasion task. Those in the Plan Question condition also devised written persuasion plans; however, once they completed their plans, the experimenter made a copy of the plan protocol and randomly selected four actions from it about which to question participants. Participants were asked what they would do in the event that the planned action failed to bring about the desired goal. As discussed previously, the questioning procedure was intended to promote the generation of alternative actions beyond those appearing in the plan protocol. Moreover, the questioning procedure should serve to raise access to planned actions. After completing this phase of the experimental induction, participants completed the persuasion task.

The action fluidity levels of the participants were determined by counting: (a) the number of vocalized pauses in their speech, (b) the frequency and duration of nonvocalized pauses, and (c) the number of false starts. In addition, two judges, blind to the experimental hypotheses and conditions, independently rated the participants' verbal fluency levels. For those who wrote plans before participating in the persuasion task the number of specific arguments they included in their plans was determined. Comparison of the three experimental conditions on the action fluidity indices revealed that the judged fluency levels of those in the Plan Question condition were significantly lower than those of the participants in the Plan Only condition. Moreover, although the differences approached but did not produce statistically significant outcomes, the pattern of means for the vocalized and nonvocalized pausing measures paralleled those of the judges' fluency judgments; however, the pattern for the false starts measure did not follow the same trend nor were there significant differences among conditions on this measure.

In order to probe further the relationships between plan complexity and action fluidity, within-condition correlations between the number of specific arguments included in the written plans and the action fluidity measures were computed. Because those individuals assigned to the No Plan condition did not produce a plan protocol, they were excluded from this analysis. The pattern of correlations showed strong support for the idea that increased plan complexity, especially under conditions of increased access (Plan Question), is related to decreased action fluidity. In the Plan Question condition, the number of specific arguments included in plan protocols was negatively related to judged verbal fluency ($r = -.62$), positively related to nonvocalized pausing ($r = .52$), positively but not significantly related to vocalized pausing ($r = .33$), and positively related to false starts in speech ($r = .43$). The four parallel correlations in the Plan Only condition were: judged verbal fluency ($r = -.26$), nonvocalized pausing ($r = .43$), vocalized pausing ($r = -.25$), and false starts ($r = -.04$). With the exception of the nonvocalized pausing correlation, none of these was statistically significant. Thus, in the Plan Question condition, there was a pervasive tendency for individuals with more specific arguments in their preinteraction plans to be less fluent verbally than those with fewer specific arguments. These relationships were generally nullified in the Plan Only condition.

A potential alternative explanation for the observed differences between the Plan Question condition and the Plan Only condition concerns the potential effects of questioning on participants' self-confidence levels. The process of questioning participants before engaging in the persuasion task could serve to undermine their self-confidence. This lowered self-confidence might, in turn, be reflected in more hesitancy in their speech during the persuasion task. Thus, the lower levels of verbal fluency observed among those in the Plan Question group might be attributable to lowered self-confidence rather than to the increased complexity of their persuasion plans. This possibility was assessed by replicating the Plan Only and Plan Question conditions. Instead of having participants participate in the persuasion task, they were asked to indicate the extent to which they felt confident that their plan would be successful in persuading another (Berger, Karol, & Jordan, 1989, Experiment 2). Analyses of these self-confidence estimates indicated no significant differences between the two groups; in fact the means of the groups were virtually identical. Thus, it does not appear that questioning individuals' plans has the effect of lowering their self-confidence in such a way that their verbal fluency might be undermined.

In general, this series of experiments provides partial support for the curvilinear formulation advanced in Proposition 10. Increasing the number of alternative actions available to interactants in the event of plan failure has the effect of reducing action fluidity, especially under conditions of increased access to planned actions. These fluency differences appear not to be mediated by such psychological states as self-confidence, and, as discussed previously, questioning plans does have the effect of inducing individuals to create unique arguments not contained in their original plans.

Assessing the Curvilinear Formulation.   Unfortunately, the experiments just described were not designed to test directly the curvilinear formulation advanced in Proposition 10. They were predicated on the notion that increased plan complexity would debilitate action fluidity in a more or less linear fashion. It was after the data for this series of experiments were collected, analyzed, and reported that the possibility of similar debilitation of action fluidity, given a paucity of alternatives, became apparent, thus resulting in the creation of Proposition 10. Consequently, additional data were collected in two experiments designed to test this hypothesized parabolic (U-curve) relationship directly (Knowlton, 1994).

In the first of these experiments, research participants were placed in the situation of providing geographic directions to another individual who, unbeknownst to the participants, was an experimental confederate. Before presenting their directions to the confederate, however, participants were assigned to one of three map preparation conditions, at which time they drew varying numbers of maps containing alternative routes for walking from the building in which the experiment was conducted to a well-known destination across campus. Specifically, participants were asked to draw either one, three, or six maps. In addition, a fourth group prepared no map in advance of providing their directions to the confederate.

After completing their maps, participants were taken to an experimental room and asked to give the confederate directions from the present location to the destination across campus. The participants did not have access to the maps they had prepared as they provided their directions to the confederate. After giving their directions, the confederates indicated that they had experienced difficulty in following the route given in the directions, and requested that the directions be provided again using an alternative route. After providing the second set of directions, participants were debriefed. The interactions were videotaped through a one-way mirror.

In this study, action fluidity was indexed by determining the amount of time that lapsed between the point at which the confederates completed indicating their misunderstanding and the point at which participants began the second rendition of their directions. As predicted by Proposition 10, individuals who had prepared either one map or six maps displayed significantly longer speech onset latencies than did their counterparts who prepared three maps. Presumably, when asked to provide an alternative walk route, those who had prepared only one map were faced with the problem of generating an alternative, and those who had prepared six maps had to choose an alternative from an extensive array of possibilities. Those who had prepared three maps most likely had to confront a choice from just two alternatives.

One finding that clouds somewhat the interpretation of these results is that the average onset latencies for the one map and six map groups did not differ significantly from that of the control group, which prepared no map prior to providing the directions; whereas those in the three-map condition took significantly less time than those in the control group to provide the second rendition of their directions. A potential implication of Proposition 10 is that those who have only a single salient alternative as they enter the direction-giving situation and those who have numerous alternatives perhaps should be more debilitated in terms of action fluidity when asked for an alternative than those who prepared no maps. However, it is also possible to conceive of the control condition as being somewhat similar to the one-map condition in that when participants in the control condition initially were asked to provide their directions, perhaps one route became highly salient to them, thus producing the kind of fixation on a single alternative that those in the one-map condition presumably experienced.

The second experiment replicated the first with one significant variation. In this experiment, individuals were given a persuasion task involving a salient campus issue to perform. This task required participants to try to persuade an experimental confederate to adopt their attitudinal position on the issue. The preparation conditions of this experiment required participants to generate either one, three, or six arguments supporting their position on the issue. As in the first study, a control group that did not prepare before the persuasion task was also included. After participants presented their first argument to the confederate, the confederate indicated that the argument was not very persuasive and asked whether the participant could present another argument on the issue. Again, speech onset latency was determined by the amount of time it took participants to begin presenting their second argument. After completing this phase of the task, participants were debriefed. In spite of the task differences between these two experiments, the onset latency results of this second experiment replicated those of the first. The same U-curve relationship was found between the number of arguments prepared and onset latency, and in this experiment, the control group onset latency was significantly less than those of the one-argument and six-argument conditions.

Although these findings are very encouraging, there is a conceptual issue regarding these experiments that should be noted. In explicating the relationships between plan complexity and action fluidity, Proposition 10 refers to plan complexity as an attribute of a specific plan to accomplish a goal rather than multiple alternative plans to attain a goal. Thus, the second experiment of this series reflects this kind of planning situation, as does the experiment described earlier that employed a similar persuasion task (Berger, Karol, & Jordan, 1989). The experiment in which individuals were required to generate alternative maps for getting from one location to another is somewhat different conceptually from the two persuasion experiments. In the direction-giving experiment, the complexity of a specific plan was not varied, but participants were required to develop alternative plans in the form of multiple maps. Thus, the complexity of a single map was not varied, although it could be by including differential amounts of detail. In spite of these conceptual differences between the two persuasion experiments and the map experiment, the consequences for action fluidity are similar: Too little or too much plan complexity is likely to reduce action fluidity when individuals are forced to resort to alternative actions in the event of plan failure.

Planning Activity and Action Fluidity

Several studies have examined the effects of generic planning activity on the subsequent fluidity of action when the plan is enacted. However, these studies typically have not related plan complexity to the fluidity with which action is performed, as the studies just reviewed have; nevertheless, they are briefly reviewed here. Greene (1984a) reported that individuals who planned discourse in advance showed reduced frequency and duration of nonvocalized pauses and speech onset latency when their plans were enacted when compared with individuals who did not plan. In a similar vein, Allen and Edwards (1991) determined that individuals who planned for an anticipated encounter displayed shorter speech onset latencies and fewer silent pauses during the actual encounter than those who were distracted from preinteraction planning.

Several studies have examined the effects of planning a deceptive act, and the display of various nonverbal behaviors when the deceptive act is perpetrated. For example, Greene, O'Hair, Cody, and Yen (1985) found that individuals who planned lies responded more quickly than those who told the truth, and deceivers who planned displayed significantly less leg/foot movement, affirmative head nodding, and head adaptors than truth-tellers. Cody, Marston, and Foster (1984) adduced evidence suggesting that those perpetrating planned lies showed fewer response latencies than those who generated spontaneous lies. Although the findings of these studies comport well with each other, some research suggests that planned lies are detected less accurately than spontaneous ones (Littlepage & Pineault, 1982), whereas other research has failed to find differences in detection accuracy between planned and spontaneous lies (DePaulo, Davis, & Lanier, 1980). Thus, within the deceptive communication domain, it appears that planning increases the fluidity with which lies are enacted; however, the relationships between planning and detection accuracy are considerably less clear. Miller and Stiff (1993) considered a number of alternative explanations for these findings.

Berger, Knowlton, and Abrahams (1996, Experiment 2) found that individuals who were given 3 minutes in which to plan a set of geographical directions demonstrated significantly faster speech rates when they gave the directions than did their counterparts who were not given time to plan; however, the speech rate differences between these two groups disappeared when participants were asked to provide a second rendition of their directions. Allen and Honeycutt (1996) contrasted the performance of individuals who planned or were distracted from planning before engaging in an interaction. They found that those who planned displayed significantly fewer object adaptors than those who were distracted from planning. Object adaptors are generally thought to reflect state anxiety.

Taken together, the results of these studies suggest that planning before engaging in social interaction is likely to increase the fluidity with which action is produced during the encounter. Although this general finding smacks of merely demonstrating the wisdom of the well-worn aphorism "Practice makes perfect," the results of those studies examining the relationship between plan complexity and action fluidity reviewed previously should give pause to those who would proffer such a glib assessment. When individuals are left to plan on their own, as they were in these studies, they devise plans that tend to facilitate their subsequent performance; however, when they devise too few or too many plans, their subsequent performance may be undermined when plan failures occur, as the studies described earlier suggest (Berger, Karol, & Jordan, 1989; Knowlton, 1994). Consequently, it is not practice per se that facilitates performance, but practice that produces plans sufficient to accomplish goals, even in the face of potential failure.

Knowledge Organization and Action Fluidity

Whereas the studies just described focused specifically on the relationship between plan complexity and action fluidity, other research has explored the relationship between knowledge organization, a construct related to plan complexity, and action fluidity (Schachter, Christenfeld, Ravina, & Bilous, 1991). These researchers argued that across various academic disciplines, knowledge tends to be organized differently. In general, knowledge in the physical and life sciences that is presented at the undergraduate level tends to be highly structured and well organized with little room for multiple interpretations. At the other extreme, within the humanities multiple interpretations of written texts and works of art are encouraged, and the level of knowledge organization within the social sciences lies between these two extremes. Another way to think about these differences is in terms of uncertainty and complexity. Given the possibilities of multiple interpretations in humanities material, the plans driving humanities professors' actions should contain more alternatives and contingencies and thus engender more uncertainty than the plans of professors in the physical and life sciences.

These differential levels of uncertainty should be reflected in the speech of professors from the various disciplines as they present lecture material; that is, the larger the number of alternative interpretations, the more likely the professors will emit filled pauses (Christenfeld, 1994). Specifically, these researchers hypothesized that when presenting lectures, humanities professors should manifest more filled pauses (um's and ah's) in their speech than professors lecturing on subjects in the physical and life sciences. Professors lecturing in social science areas should show filled pause rates intermediate between these extremes. To test this hypothesis, students attended large lecture classes across these disciplines and recorded the number of filled pauses professors manifested during their lectures. In addition, under the guise of conducting a faculty survey, other students interviewed the same professors in their offices, who had been observed during their lectures, about topics unrelated to their field of study. These latter data were collected to control for the possibility that any differential rates of filled pauses observed among the disciplines were not the result of self-selection factors. For example, it is possible that for some unknown reason individuals who select themselves into the physical and life sciences might be more verbally fluent than those who choose careers in the humanities.

The results of this study revealed that lecturers in the physical and life sciences demonstrated filled pause rates that were significantly lower than those manifested by social scientists. In turn, the filled pause rates of the social scientist lecturers were significantly lower than those of professors lecturing in the humanities. Furthermore, the filled pause rates among these three groups were not significantly different from each other in the interview context, thus suggesting that the differences observed among the disciplines most likely are not due to self-selection factors that have nothing to do with the organization of knowledge of the disciplines. If one grants the possibility that an attribute underlying the differences in knowledge organization among the disciplines has something to do with plan complexity, the results of this study can be taken as at least indirect support for the idea that increasingly complex plans tend to produce reductions in the fluidity of the actions guided by them.

Access to Planned Actions and Action Fluidity

Although there are no data bearing directly on Proposition 11, which predicts displacement of the U-curve upward as access to planned actions increases, there is some evidence to support the more general claim that greater access to planned actions increases the fluidity with which they are enacted during social interaction episodes. This more general proposition does not take into account differential plan complexity. In this context access refers to the speed with which alternative planned actions can be retrieved. It is one thing to have a plan available in memory, it is quite another to be able to retrieve rapidly the actions contained in the plan.

This general relationship was assessed in a study in which individuals each wrote two different plans for persuading another person to adopt their position on two different attitude issues (Berger, 1988c). After completing their persuasion plans, an experimenter copied them and selected all of the actions from each plan that could be questioned. Participants were then questioned concerning what they would do if they enacted each of the actions but they failed to bring about the desired result, the same procedure as that used by Berger, Karol, and Jordan (1989, Experiment 1). These interviews were tape recorded. One week later, under the guise of a different study, participants returned to the laboratory and were given the task of persuading an experimental confederate to adopt their position on one of the two issues for which they had planned during the previous week's session.

Judges unfamiliar with the hypotheses and purposes of the study independently viewed each interaction and judged the verbal fluency of each participant on a series of 7-point scales. Other judges listened to the tapes of the interviews during which participants' persuasion plans were questioned. As part of this process, they recorded the amount of time that lapsed between the point at which the interviewer finished asking what the participant would do in the event of an action's failure and the point at which the participant began to answer the question. These latencies then were averaged for each plan.

Given the design of this study, it was possible to compute the correlations between the mean latencies for the questioned planned actions and the level of verbal fluency both for the attitude issue that ultimately was argued during the persuasion task and the attitude issue that was planned for and questioned in the first session but not argued one week later. The correlation between the mean response latency and fluency for the issue argued was $-.36$ ($p < .001$). By contrast, the correlation between mean response latency for the issue not argued and fluency was $.04$ (ns). The two correlations differed significantly ($Z = 2.17$, $p < .05$). These correlations demonstrate two important points. The first correlation provides support for the claim that more rapid access to planned actions is related to increased verbal fluency, thus supporting the hypothesis based on Proposition 11. The nonsignificant correlation between mean latencies for the issue not argued and verbal fluency based on the issue argued, combined with the fact that this correlation was significantly less than the first correlation, indicates that rapid access to planned actions in one attitude domain does not readily generalize to performance in another attitude domain. Apparently, rapidity of access is domain specific.

Although not directly concerned with Proposition 11, two other findings of this study are worth noting. As described previously, the level of involvement in each of the attitude issues used in this study was determined by computing the degree to which each participant's position on each issue deviated from the neutral position on the scale on which they indicated their own position on the issue. This involvement measure, which was taken during the first session, was found to be positively related to the fluency with which they argued on the issue one week later ($r = .26$, $p < .02$). Moreover, the involvement measure also correlated negatively with the latency with which individuals provided answers to the interviewer's questions about alternative actions that might be taken in the event of plan failure ($r = -.22$,

$p < .04$), those with higher involvement levels displayed shorter latencies in answering the questions. Thus, access to both alternative actions and action fluidity were influenced by the degree to which individuals were involved in the attitude issues. More generally, because it was suggested earlier that attitude involvement might be a surrogate for goal desire, these findings could be recast with respect to that theoretical variable.

SUMMARY

In this chapter the antecedents and consequences of plan complexity were considered. Individuals who have a propensity to value planning as an activity, those with high levels of self-monitoring, and people with high levels of cognitive complexity are more likely to develop complex plans. In addition, having high levels of goal desire, directly questioning planned actions, and thinking about the people and situations within which plans will be enacted promote higher levels of plan complexity. Although considerable evidence suggests that planning generally promotes action fluidity, additional evidence indicates that when plans fail, the type of plan being utilized also influences the fluidity with which action is produced. Specifically, individuals with very simple plans and those with highly complex plans tend to exhibit lower levels of action fluidity than individuals with moderate plan complexity levels when their plans are thwarted and they must search for alternative actions for reaching desired goals. Finally, individuals with more rapid access to planned actions tend to show higher levels of action fluidity.

Chapter 4

The Hierarchy Principle

᳄   ◆   ᳄

This chapter deals with an extremely significant problem that humans as planners and social agents often confront. No matter how carefully plans to achieve goals are developed and mentally simulated before they are acted out in the crucible of social interaction, the future always presents some measure of uncertainty, thus raising the probability of plan failure to some value greater than zero in almost all social situations. This is not to say that when plan failures occur, they are necessarily catastrophic and undermine the entire plan. To the contrary, it is likely that when these failures take place, they involve only certain parts of plans. Once these specific subplans are modified, the overall plan may be carried out without further difficulty. Nevertheless, whether plan failure is limited in scope or highly pervasive, individuals who wish to continue to pursue their goals in the face of such adversity must somehow alter their plans to circumvent the countervailing circumstances they have encountered. In dealing with these processes, this chapter takes it as a given that when individuals are faced with plan failures, their goal desire is of sufficient strength to induce them to continue their goal attainment efforts. This postulate is an obvious necessity, if one wishes to study the effects of plan failure on subsequent planning activities.

Throughout the following presentation it is important to keep in mind that understanding how people surmount plan failures is not only important from the point of view of ultimate strategic success; it also is probably the case that we learn most about our own and others' capabilities when these failures must be overcome. Immediate success in reaching a desired goal indicates that the successful individual had a plan of sufficient quality and the necessary performative acumen to reach the goal in question; however, observing such instances of immediate success does not provide us with information about the breadth and depth of the individual's plan repertoire. It is only when the person fails and continues to pursue the desired goal that we obtain some estimate of the planning and performative resources at the person's disposal. Although this particular issue is not the focus of the present chapter, it certainly deserves serious research attention. It is an excellent paradigm for learning more about both planning abilities and performative competence.

THE HIERARCHY PRINCIPLE

As discussed in chapter 2 in connection with Proposition 6 and its two corollaries, the Hierarchy Principle lies at the confluence of several postulates. The first of these is that humans have limited abilities to processes all of the relevant information available to them at any given point in time (Hogarth, 1980; Kahneman, Slovic, & Tversky, 1982; Nisbett & Ross, 1980). A second and related postulate is that people are prone to select the least effortful means for processing information (Fiske & Taylor, 1984, 1991). This postulate does not preclude the possibility that people will choose to devote considerable resources to information processing; however, it implies that individuals are biased toward minimizing information-processing effort. Third, both theory and research reviewed in chapter 2 suggested that plans are hierarchically organized knowledge structures with more abstract plan units at the tops of these hierarchies. Fourth, alterations to the more abstract units located at the tops of these hierarchies require more effort to implement than do low-level modifications. Changes in more abstract units cascade down the plan hierarchy, thus requiring realignment of lower level plan units. By contrast, alterations of low-level units do not necessarily imply changes in more abstract plan units. The shift in attention from higher to lower level plan units in response to goal failure postulated here bears some resemblance to a central assumption of action identification theory (Vallacher & Wegner, 1985; Vallacher, Wegner, & Somoza, 1989); however, their theory does not deal directly with alterations to message plan hierarchies.

Taken together, these four postulates generate the hierarchy principle as articulated in Proposition 6: "When people experience thwarting internal to the interaction, their first response is likely to involve low level plan hierarchy alterations. Continued thwarting will tend to produce more abstract alterations to plan hierarchies."

Although not based on this particular line of theoretical reasoning, Ringle and Bruce (1980) argued that when communication failures occur during conversations, individuals are most likely to assume that the failures are acoustically based rather than the result of some potentially more complex problem. Perhaps the least demanding way to respond to comprehension failures during conversation is to repeat what has just been said, but say it in a louder voice. This is precisely the kind of strategy the hierarchy principle would suggest because vocal intensity is among the lower level plan attributes that could be altered, and repeating what has just been said avoids the necessity of altering more abstract message plan attributes. In contrast to increasing vocal amplitude in response to communication failure, it takes considerably more time and energy to modify such higher level plan attributes as sentence structure, the order in which sentences are uttered, and the content of utterances. In a similar vein, parents attempting to induce behavioral compliance in their recalcitrant children may repeat what they have said during previous influence attempts but change such easily altered, low-level plan attributes as vocal intensity, vocal intonation, and speech rate, as they continue to try to influence their resistant children.

The hierarchy principle does not imply that individuals will invariably choose low-level plan unit alterations over more abstract ones, as the two corollaries to Proposition 6 indicate. People with elevated goal desire levels should be more willing to expend the cognitive resources necessary to make more abstract plan modifications in the face of repeated failure. Furthermore, these individuals should be prone to initiate higher level changes earlier in a failure sequence than their counterparts with lower goal desire levels. For instance, individuals with a high level of desire to persuade another may be more likely to restructure the content of their persuasive messages when their initial message plans fail, and to make such alterations earlier in a continuing sequence of message exchanges between themselves and their targets than will their less desirous counterparts. As yet, there have been no direct tests of these two corollaries to the hierarchy principle; consequently, the remainder of this chapter focuses on tests of the principle itself and sets aside the question of goal-desire effects.

ASSESSING THE HIERARCHY PRINCIPLE

A number of studies have addressed the potential validity of the hierarchy principle. Among these studies are several that were designed to test the principle directly, whereas another study to be considered provides an indirect test of the principle. All of these studies employed an experimental paradigm in which individuals involved in communication situations experienced some kind of communication failure, (e.g., noncomprehension). In some of the studies, differential responses to these failures were taken as evidence for alterations of message-plan hierarchies at various levels. A somewhat different approach to assessing the plausibility of the hierarchy principle is to manipulate the locus of communication failure in such a way that the basis of the failure itself is located at different levels of the message-plan hierarchy. If the postulates underlying the hierarchy principle are sound, then ameliorating failures at lower levels of the hierarchy should be less demanding of cognitive resources than repairing failures at more abstract levels; that is, higher level alterations to message-plan hierarchies should place planner-communicators under a greater cognitive load than would lower level modifications. These cognitive load studies are considered after examining experiments that have explored the propensity for individuals to alter message plans spontaneously at various hierarchical levels in response to communication failure.

Studies of Spontaneous Message Plan Alterations

Effects of Distorted Communication.   Although not designed as an explicit test of the hierarchy principle, the results of a study reported by Longhurst and Siegel (1973) are relevant to it. In this experiment, research participants worked on a referential communication task while communicating over an electronic communication system. As the participants performed the task, various levels of distortion were introduced into the circuit linking the participants, such that several words at a time were rendered unintelligible. In response to this interference, message senders decreased their speech rate and increased the length of their descriptions. Anecdotal evidence suggested that the message senders also increased their levels of vocal intensity as distortion levels increased; however, no systematic measures of vocal intensity were reported.

Assuming the validity of the anecdotal observations, at least two of the communication parameters on which research participants showed changes in response to the distortion—namely speech rate and vocal intensity—could be considered low-level message-plan attributes. The inclusion of more detail in the descriptions is most certainly a higher level, more demanding message plan alteration; however, it is difficult to determine exactly how much higher in the message plan hierarchy this particular message attribute is. That is, it is not clear whether the message senders in this study reformulated their descriptions entirely (i.e., a very high-level modification) or whether they simply added detail to an already formulated description, a somewhat less cognitively demanding task. Nevertheless, as these findings stand, they provide tentative support for the claim that thwarted message senders show a propensity to make lower level modifications to message plans when faced with communication failure.

If at First You Don't Succeed, Say It Louder and Slower.   In a study designed explicitly with the hierarchy principle in mind, participants were given the task of providing geographic directions from the laboratory in which the study was taking place to a well-known destination (an elevated train station) located some distance from the laboratory (Berger & diBattista, 1993). Experimental confederates, some of whom were Asian and some of whom were Caucasian, indicated their inability to follow the directions after the direction givers completed the first rendition of their directions. At this point, a second factor was varied. In half of the cases the confederates indicated that the reason they could not follow the directions was because the directions themselves were not clear. To reassure participants, confederates also indicated that their difficulty in following the directions had nothing to do with their level of English proficiency. In a second experimental condition, confederates told other direction givers that the reason they could not follow the directions was because they could not speak or understand English well. Confederates delivered this experimental induction using a very thick accent. The Asian confederates, who were natives of Singapore and Taiwan, affected accents appropriate to speakers of their languages, and the Caucasian confederates affected Eastern European-sounding accents. After confederates indicated their inability to follow the first set of directions, participants provided a second rendition of the directions.

The two renditions of the directions were compared to determine the hierarchical levels at which message plan alterations were made. The most demanding alteration to the message plans underlying the directions would be to reformulate them completely by providing a new route in the second rendition. A somewhat less demanding modification would be to reiterate the same route in the second rendition but to add such details as landmarks to the descriptions. Because individuals primarily used buildings as landmarks, the number of buildings included in each set of directions was determined. Finally, the lowest level and least cognitively demanding message plan alterations would be those associated with such communication parameters as speech rate and vocal intensity. Intercorrelations among the route change, number of buildings per words, speech rate, and vocal intensity indicators revealed significant autocorrelations between renditions for the latter three measures; of course, it was not possible to compute a correlation across time for the route-change index. The only other significant correlation observed was between the route-change index and buildings/words at time 2 ($r = .26, p < .01$); those who changed their routes tended to include more buildings in the second rendition of their directions. However, outside of this very modest correlation, all other correlations among the four measures were nonsignificant; thus, separate analyses were conducted for each measure.

In general, the results of this study provided considerable support for the hierarchy principle. First, of the 96 study participants, only 5.20% spontaneously altered the walk route they provided in the second rendition of their directions. The lack of change in this attribute across renditions is understandable in the case of those who were faced with a confederate who indicated limited ability to understand English; however, for the half of the participants who were told that the locus of the comprehension problem was the directions themselves, one would expect more route changes to be made in the second rendition. Thus, across all of the conditions of this experiment, virtually no high-level message plan alterations were made by study participants.

Changes at the next lower hierarchy level were indexed by computing the number of buildings included in each rendition of the directions and dividing that number by the number of words in the description in order to control for message length. A 2 x 2 x 2 analysis of variance (ANOVA) of this index employing confederate race and locus of communication failure as between-subjects factors, and rendition as a within-subjects factor revealed only a main effect for rendition, $F(1, 92) = 8.48, p < .004$. Across the four experimental conditions, participants included significantly fewer buildings in the second rendition of their directions than they did in the first. Thus, there was a tendency for direction givers to simplify the directions they provided after experiencing communication failure. Interestingly, this tendency was no more pronounced in the condition in which confederates indicated a lack of ability to understand English well.

Finally, there was evidence of alterations to both low-level message-plan attributes. Vocal intensity and speech rate were analyzed separately in the same 2 x 2 x 2 ANOVA design as was the buildings/words index. Measures of participants' vocal intensity taken from the tapes of the interactions revealed that across all of the experimental conditions, participants spoke significantly louder during the second rendition than they did during the first rendition of their directions ($F(1, 92) = 5.96, p < .02$). No other main effects or interactions were significant. Furthermore, analysis of the speech rate parameter showed that participants also spoke more slowly during the second rendition of their directions; however, unlike the vocal intensity parameter, this main effect was qualified by a triple interaction among rendition, confederate race, and locus of communication failure, $F(1, 92) = 4.73, p < .032$. This complex interaction was due primarily to the drastic decrease in speech rate for participants who gave their directions to White confederates who indicated inability to understand English well, $t(92) = 2.12, p < .05$. This complex interaction was explained by recourse to the notion that participants, most of whom were themselves White, simply did not expect to encounter language-based communication failure when interacting with a White confederate, a supposition that manipulation check data supported. Moreover, crucial to this explanation is the fact that while participants delivered the first rendition of their directions, they were unaware of the linguistic status of the confederate, because no verbal interaction between them was permitted before the first rendition of the directions was delivered.

Although the results of this study comport well with the hierarchy principle, there is at least one ambiguity in the findings that should be addressed. This issue involves the landmarks measure. In this case, it is not clear whether reducing the number of buildings from the first to the second rendition of the directions, as occurred in this experiment, is any more or less cognitively demanding than adding landmarks to the directions across renditions. The fact that alterations of any kind were made at this hierarchical level indicates that at least some individuals were willing to move up the hierarchy and make more cognitively demanding changes in their message plans; however, it would be useful to know if the kind of message simplification observed in this experiment is more, less, or no more taxing on the cognitive system than adding details to the message plan, as was apparently the case in the Longhurst and Siegel (1973) study. Additional research effort will be necessary to answer this question directly.

Finally, it is clear from both this experiment and the Longhurst and Siegel (1973) study that the message plan adaptations that individuals make in response to communication failure are not necessarily functional for overcoming the problem. Given the types of communication failures used in these studies, it is difficult to see how increasing vocal intensity would have been a particularly useful strategy for making oneself understood. Even in the case of Longhurst and Siegel's (1973) study, which employed a physical source of interference, the distortion introduced into the communication system over which research participants interacted had the effect of deleting groups of words, not lowering the vocal intensities of the speakers. Furthermore, my conversations with a number of English as a Second Language (ESL) teachers have revealed that even those with considerable experience in teaching English to nonnative English speakers tend to raise their vocal intensity levels when their students fail to understand them, in spite of the fact that they are well aware of this tendency and recognize its futility for making themselves understood. This kind of automatic response to diverse types of communication failures suggests that increasing vocal intensity in response to not being understood may be a default option activated when communication failures of most kinds occur. Of course, because increasing vocal intensity does not demand many cognitive resources, making this an "automatic default" in the event of most communication failures does not exact a very high price on the cognitive economy, and it serves to cover the contingency of not being heard the second time, if the locus of the communication failure is acoustically based.

Time Constraint Effects.   A follow-up experiment to the previous study was conducted to determine whether introducing time constraints to the direction-giving task would induce people to make alterations at different levels of the message plan hierarchy (Berger & diBattista, 1992b). Specifically, it was predicted that individuals communicating under time constraints would be less likely than their nonconstrained counterparts to make higher level alterations to message plans when they encountered communication failure. People interacting under no time constraints should be more prone to make higher level alterations.

The time constraint manipulation was introduced before research participants gave their directions the first time. One third of the research participants were informed that they would be given one minute to give their directions. Another third of the participants was told they would be given 3 minutes to give their directions. The final group in this experiment was not placed under any external time constraint. The same direction-giving task was employed in this study; however, unlike the previous experiment, the locus of communication failure was held constant. In this study, after participants delivered the first rendition of their directions to the experimental confederates, the confederates simply informed the participants that they had difficulty following them. The participants then gave the second rendition of their directions. Participants all were given as much time as was necessary to complete both renditions of their directions.

It was reasoned that introducing time constraints into the direction-giving task should have the overall effect of inducing individuals to speak for shorter periods of time. As a manipulation check, speaking times and the numbers of words spoken were employed as dependent variables in two separate analyses. These analyses showed that across both renditions of their directions, participants in the One Minute condition spoke for significantly ($p < .05$) shorter amounts of time (M = 37.75s) than their counterparts in the other two conditions, overall $F(2, 46) = 4.36$, $p < .02$; however, those in the Three Minute condition (M = 61.72s) did not differ significantly from those in the No Constraint condition (M = 58.24s). The same pattern of differences among the three conditions was evidenced for the number of words uttered; however, these differences fell just short of conventional significance levels. As in the previous experiment, route changes, buildings/words, speech rate, and vocal intensity were used to index plan alterations at decreasingly abstract message plan hierarchy levels. These indicators were not significantly correlated.

Consistent with the previous experiment, participants in this study did not respond to the communication failure by altering the walk route used in their directions. Only 4.08% of the 49 participants demonstrated route changes, a figure that is very close to the proportion observed in the previous study. Given the rarity with which spontaneous route changes were made, it was not possible to contrast route-change rates among the experimental conditions. However, it was possible to contrast the conditions on the somewhat less abstract buildings/words index. Here, some support for the theoretical hypothesis was found. Specifically, across both renditions, participants who gave their directions under no time constraints included significantly more ($p < .05$) buildings in their directions than did individuals who communicated under either of the two time constraint conditions, overall $F(2, 46) = 4.33$, $p < .02$. Furthermore, there was no significant difference on this index between the two time constraint conditions. Although no significant differences were observed among the conditions across the two renditions with respect to speech rate, the vocal intensity parameter did show significant differences. Across all conditions combined, there was a significant increase in vocal intensity during the second rendition of the directions, a result that replicates those of the previous experiment, $F(1, 46) = 7.22$, $p < .01$. Moreover, across both renditions of the directions combined, those given 3 minutes to provide their directions showed significantly higher ($p < .05$) vocal intensity levels than those in the other two conditions, whereas the other two conditions did not differ significantly from each other with respect to this speech parameter, overall $F(2, 46) = 3.21$, $p < .003$.

Although this latter result is difficult to explain in terms of the logic of the hierarchy principle, the overall pattern of findings lends support to the idea that time constraints tend to discourage planners from making higher level message plan alterations when they experience communication failure. In this regard, it is of interest to note that although those individuals given 3 minutes to deliver their directions spoke for significantly longer periods of time than participants who were given only 1 minute to render their directions, like their more highly constrained counterparts, those given 3 minutes included significantly fewer buildings in their descriptions than those who communicated without externally imposed time constraints. Thus, even though a time constraint effect did not manifest itself in the speaking times of those in the Three Minute condition, it was evident in the tendency for participants to cope with the time constraint by reducing the level of cognitively demanding details they included in both renditions of their directions.

The fact that speech rate remained unaffected by the manipulations of the present experiment is of considerable interest. Recall that in the previous experiment, participants who gave directions to a White person who indicated difficulty understanding English showed significant decreases in speech rate during the second rendition of their directions. The lack of change in speech rate across renditions of the present experiment may reflect the fact that no evidence for language-based communication failure was provided to participants. All of the confederates spoke English as a first language. Consequently, it may be that extremely severe levels of communication failure are necessary, such as those associated with not speaking a language at all or not speaking it very well, before individuals will lower their speech rate when trying to repair a communication breakdown.

The findings of this study have implications for understanding how individuals' communication is affected when they attempt to reach social goals under time constraints. For example, if parents see their unsuspecting child in the path of an oncoming vehicle, they are likely to utter a very simple message in an extremely loud voice. Of course, in this particular example, extreme levels of affect may partially explain these message choices. Nevertheless, even in less dramatic everyday examples, time constraints frequently act to simplify message content and may have the effect of influencing such paralinguistic message features as vocal intensity.

Message Plan Hierarchy Levels and Cognitive Load

An important, yet untested supposition underlying the three studies discussed here is that alterations to abstract levels of message-plan hierarchies are more demanding of scarce cognitive resources than are lower level modifications. Although the studies just described demonstrate a bias in the direction of lower level alterations, they do not provide direct support for the differential cognitive load explanation of these preference patterns. Consequently, the following series of experiments was undertaken to test directly this critical postulate underlying the hierarchy principle and to determine whether, in the spirit of the falsificationist credo (Greenwald, Pratkanis, Leippe, & Baumgardner, 1986; Popper, 1969), the postulate might be subverted under certain conditions.

Failure Locus, Time Constraint, and Cognitive Load. This initial attempt to assess the veracity of the general hypothesis that modifications of higher-level attributes of message-plan hierarchies are more cognitively demanding than lower level alterations to hierarchies was tested in an experiment in which direction givers were told by experimental confederates that their directions could not be understood for different reasons (Berger, Knowlton, & Abrahams, 1996, Experiment 1). After providing the first rendition of their directions, participants in the Δ-Speech Rate condition were told that the directions were not understood because the participants spoke too quickly. Confederates asked participants to speak more slowly while giving the second rendition of their directions. By contrast, participants in the Δ-Route condition were informed that the reason their directions were difficult to understand was the route they used. These participants were asked to provide another route in the second rendition of their directions. Individuals assigned to the third condition of this locus of communication failure manipulation simply were told that the directions were difficult to understand. When providing feedback in this Unspecified Failure condition, confederates used the same wording to express their lack of understanding as was used in the previous experiment. In addition to this locus of communication failure manipulation, time constraint was again varied. In this study, half of the participants were placed under the same 1 minute time constraint as were participants in the previous experiment, and the other half of the participants were not placed under any external time constraint; however, all experimental participants were allowed as much time as they needed to finish the task. Cognitive load was indexed by determining the amount of time it took each participant to begin providing the second rendition of their directions after receiving the feedback from the confederate.

If the reasoning underlying the hierarchy hypothesis is correct, individuals in the Δ-Route condition should manifest longer speech onset latencies than their counterparts in the Δ-Speech Rate condition, because changing the walk route in a set of directions is a higher level message-plan alteration than is changing speech rate. Furthermore, since individuals are prone to assume that communication failures arising from unspecified sources are due to acoustical failures—the amelioration of which involve lower level changes in vocal intensity (Ringle & Bruce, 1980)—onset latencies similar to those observed in the Δ-Speech Rate condition would be expected in the Unspecified Failure condition. Overall, those communicating under time constraints should show shorter speech onset latencies than those interacting under no constraints; however, this differential should be most pronounced among those in the Δ-Route condition, who are asked to make higher level message-plan alterations. This line of reasoning suggests an interaction between locus of communication failure and time constraint on speech onset latency.

To determine the effectiveness of the time constraint manipulation, a 3 x 2 x 2 ANOVA was computed using locus of communication failure and time constraint as between-subjects factors, and rendition as a within-subjects factor with speaking time as the dependent variable. As was observed in the previous experiment, participants communicating under the one-minute time constraint spoke for significantly shorter periods of time (M = 49.27s) during both renditions of the directions combined than did those individuals communicating under no external time constraint (M = 76.26s), thus suggesting the effectiveness of the time constraint manipulation, $F(1,121) = 13.17$, $p < .0001$. No other main effects or interaction effects were significant in this analysis. Moreover, in contrast to the 88.10% of those in the Δ-Route condition who provided a different route when giving the second rendition of their directions, no participants in the Δ-Speech Rate condition changed their walk routes across renditions, and only 2.50% of those in the Unspecified Failure condition spontaneously altered the walk route in the second rendition of the directions, $\chi^2(2) = 96.02$, $p < .00001$.

An analysis of the speech rate parameter (words/sec.) using the same 3 x 2 x 2 ANOVA design yielded a significant interaction only between locus of communication failure and rendition, $F(2,121) = 3.52$, $p < .04$. Decomposition of this interaction using simple effects tests found that within the Unspecified Failure condition, those in the One Minute condition spoke significantly faster (M = 2.83 words/seconds) than those in the Unconstrained condition (M = 2.38 words/second), $t(121) = 3.09$, $p < .01$. By contrast, within the Δ-Speech Rate and Δ-Route conditions, there were no significant differences in speech rate between the two time constraint groups. Moreover, there was no significant change in speech rate among those participants in the Δ-Speech Rate condition across renditions, even though these individuals were asked explicitly to speak more slowly.

The means and standard deviations for the speech onset latency data are presented in Table 4.1. Given the obvious heterogeneity of variances among the conditions, a log_{10} transformation (Kirk, 1968; Winer, 1971) was applied to the speech onset latency scores and an ANOVA was computed. This analysis showed a significant main effect for locus of communication failure and no other statistically significant effects, $F(2,121) = 11.39$, $p < .0001$, $\eta^2 = .16$. Newman-Keuls follow-up tests revealed that the speech onset latency for the Δ-Route condition was significantly greater ($p < .05$) than each of the means of the other two conditions, and that the means for the other two conditions were not significantly different from each other. Although the mean onset latency for the One Minute group was less than the mean for the group communicating under no time constraints, and the discrepancy between the two time constraint groups' means within the Δ-Route condition was greater than that observed for the other two conditions as predicted, this main effect and interaction effect failed to reach conventional levels of statistical significance.

In general, the results of this experiment support the notion that alterations to message plan hierarchies at more abstract levels are more demand-

TABLE 4.1

Mean Speech Onset Latency in Seconds

	Locus of Communication Failure		
	Unspecified Failure	Δ-Speech Rate	Δ-Route
Time Constraint			
No Constraint	5.98	3.69	9.77
	(12.29)	(2.19)	(7.14)
	n=22	n=21	n=22
One Minute	3.99	3.27	5.63
	(3.61)	(2.73)	(3.85)
	n=20	n=19	n=23
Total	5.03	3.49	7.65
	(9.19)	(2.44)	(6.01)
	n=42	n=40	n=45

Note. Standard deviations appear in parentheses. Table adapted from Berger, Knowlton, and Abrahams (1996, Experiment 1). Reprinted with permission from Guilford Press.

ing of scarce cognitive resources than are modifications at lower levels in the hierarchy. These data also hint at the possibility that time constraints may act to dampen the differences in cognitive load among hierarchical levels. Further work is necessary to determine whether the interaction pattern observed in this experiment can be replicated in a study with somewhat greater statistical power.

Failure Locus, Planning, and Cognitive Load.   Because the Δ-Speech Rate and Δ-Route conditions of the previous experiment represented polar extremes of the message plan hierarchy, a second experiment was conducted that included both of these conditions, as well as a condition designed to require modifications at intermediate hierarchical levels (Berger et al., 1996, Experiment 2). In this intermediate condition labeled Δ-Landmarks, participants were asked to provide more landmarks in the second rendition of their directions, after being told that their directions were difficult to follow because they did not contain enough landmarks. Providing more landmarks did not require direction givers to make the more demanding plan alteration of changing the walk route, but it did require adding details to the previous description, clearly a more demanding task than reiterating the message at a higher level of vocal intensity. Consequently, it was predicted that the speech onset latency between the two renditions for the Δ-Landmarks condition should fall between those of the Δ-Speech Rate and Δ-Route conditions.

In addition to this augmented locus of communication failure manipulation, a second factor was varied in this experiment. Because previous research (Greene, 1984a) demonstrated that planning before engaging in speaking tends to increase speech fluency, a planning manipulation was introduced into the design. Theoretically, in the context of the direction-giving task, individuals given time to prepare their directions in advance should be more fluent when delivering the first rendition; however, advanced preparation should have the effect of fixating direction givers on one route. Consequently, when direction givers in the)-Route condition who have planned are asked to provide another route, their onset latency should be significantly greater than those participants who did not plan their directions in advance. These onset latency differentials between planners and nonplanners should not manifest themselves in the two conditions requiring lower level modifications to message plans, thus implying an interaction between the locus of communication failure and planning variables. The locus of communication failure manipulation was carried out in exactly the same way as it was in the previous experiment with the addition of the)-Landmarks condition. The planning manipulation was instantiated by giving half the participants 3 minutes in which to plan a route before they provided their directions to experimental confederates. The other half of the participants was given no time in which to plan their directions.

Because 88.46% of the participants in the Δ-Route condition and only 7.41% and 7.69% of the participants in the Δ-Speech Rate and Δ-Landmarks conditions respectively changed the walk route in their directions across renditions, the evidence is overwhelming that the Δ-Route manipulation was successful, $\chi^2(2) = 50.76$, $p < .00001$. To determine whether those in the Δ-Landmarks condition actually increased the number of landmarks in the second rendition of their directions, the number of landmarks appearing in each rendition of the directions was determined. In this case, landmarks not only included buildings but such geographic markers as parking lots, pig sties, monuments, signs, and groves of trees. To control for differences in message length, the number of landmarks in each message rendition was divided by the total number of words uttered during that rendition. These ratios were contrasted in a 3 x 2 x 2 ANOVA employing locus of communication and planning as between-subjects factors and rendition as a within-subjects factor. This analysis yielded a significant main effect for locus of communication failure, $F(2,73) = 4.03$, $p < .03$, and a significant rendition main effect, $F(1,73) = 5.62$, $p < .02$. However, these main effects were qualified by a significant locus of communication failure by rendition interaction, $F(2,73) = 18.54$, $p < .0001$. Simple main effects tests were conducted to determine the source of this interaction. They showed that within the Δ-Speech Rate and Δ-Route conditions there was no significant change in the landmarks/words ratios across renditions; however, within the Δ-Landmarks condition there was a significant increase in these ratios, $M_{t1} = 12.23$, $M_{t2} = 20.54$, $t(72) = 14.66$, $p < .001$. These analyses demonstrate that only those in the Δ-Landmarks condition significantly increased the number of landmarks included in the second rendition of their directions. Finally, a 3 x 2 x 2 ANOVA of speech rates (words/second) produced a significant interaction only between the planning and rendition factors, $F(1,73) = 9.40$, $p < .003$. This analysis indicates that there was no significant differential tendency for those in the Δ-Speech Rate condition to change their rate of speech across renditions when compared with those participants in the other two locus of communication failure conditions.

Table 4.2 contains the speech onset latency data germane to the main hypothesis of the experiment. Again, because the variances were heterogeneous, a $\log_{10}$ transformation was applied to the speech onset latency scores and a 3 x 2 ANOVA was computed using locus of communication failure and planning as between subjects factors. This analysis produced a significant main effect for locus of communication failure, $F(2,73) = 19.07$, $p < .0001$, $\eta^2 = .33$. Neither the other main effect nor the interaction effect reached significant levels. A Newman-Keuls test was conducted to compare the three locus of communication failure conditions. Consistent with the first hypothesis, this test revealed that the mean latency for the Δ-Route condition ($M = 13.04s$) was significantly ($p < .05$) greater than the mean

TABLE 4.2

Mean Speech Onset Latency in Seconds

	Locus of Communication Failure		
	Δ-Speech Rate	Δ-Landmarks	Δ-Route
Planning			
Yes	3.18	5.92	13.67
	(1.57)	(3.97)	(12.61)
	n=13	n=14	n=13
No	3.28	4.21	12.41
	(1.52)	(3.97)	(9.06)
	n=14	n=12	n=13
Total	3.23	5.13	13.04
	(1.51)	(3.98)	(10.77)
	n=27	n=26	n=26

Note. Standard deviations appear in parentheses.

Table adapted from Berger, Knowlton, and Abrahams (1996, Experiment 2). Reprinted with permission from Guilford Press.

latencies for the Δ-Landmarks (M = 5.13s) and the Δ-Speech Rate (M = 3.23s) conditions. As predicted, the mean speech onset latency for the Δ-Landmarks condition was greater than the mean observed for the Δ-Speech Rate condition; however, the comparison between these two means fell just short of conventional significance levels. An ANOVA computed on the untransformed speech latency scores produced the same pattern of results.

Because a modest discrepancy between the smallest and largest variances remained even after applying the $\log_{10}$ transformation, as a precaution, a nonparametric Kruskal-Wallis one-way ANOVA was computed on the speech onset latency scores using locus of communication failure as the independent variable. This analysis revealed a significant overall difference among the three conditions, $\chi^2(2) = 22.53$, $p < .00001$. In addition, Mann-Whitney U tests were conducted on pairs of conditions. These comparisons again demonstrated that the speech onset latencies observed in the Δ-Route condition were greater than those observed in both the Δ-Landmarks condition (Z = 3.23, $p < .0006$) and the Δ-Speech Rate condition (Z=4.48, $p < .000005$). Moreover, in this analysis the speech onset latencies for the Δ-Landmarks condition proved to be significantly greater than those observed in the Δ-Speech Rate condition (Z = 1.75, $p < .04$). Thus, these nonparametric analyses lend unqualified support to the main hypothesis.

A potential qualification of the main hypothesis was suggested by asserting that preinteraction planning would increase the cognitive load placed on those who were asked to make high-level message plan alterations, that is, route changes. By contrast, message planning activity before interaction would produce little impact on cognitive load for those asked to make lower level alterations to message plans. Although the pattern of speech onset latencies shown in Table 4.2 is consistent with this hypothesis, because the analyses presented here found no evidence of a significant interaction between locus of communication failure and planning on speech onset latencies, there is no support for this interaction hypothesis.

The second hypothesis suggested that because preinteraction planning facilitates verbal fluency (Greene, 1984a), those who had planned their route before the interaction should speak more rapidly than those who did not engage in planning, at least during the first rendition of their directions. This hypothesis was tested by computing the 3 x 2 x 2 ANOVA of the speech rate scores using locus of communication failure and planning as between-subjects factors and rendition as a within-subjects factor, as described previously. The means and standard deviations of the speech rate measure are shown in Table 4.3. This analysis yielded a significant planning by rendition interaction, $F(1,73) = 9.40, p < .003$, but no additional significant main effects or interactions. The significant interaction between planning and rendition was decomposed using simple main effects tests. These tests showed that during the first rendition of the directions, those who planned showed a significantly higher rate of speech (words/second; M = 2.89 words/second) than those who did not plan in advance (M = 2.29

TABLE 4.3

Means for Speech Rate in Words per Second

| | Locus of Communication Failure | | | | | |
| | Δ-Speech Rate | | Δ-Landmarks | | Δ-Route | |
	No Plan	Plan	No Plan	Plan	No Plan	Plan
Rendition						
First	2.33	3.31	2.38	2.65	2.19	2.69
	(.67)	(1.61)	(.69)	(.78)	(.66)	(.84)
	$n=14$	$n=13$	$n=12$	$n=14$	$n=13$	$n=13$
Second	2.50	2.62	2.62	2.39	2.25	2.43
	(.62)	(.66)	(.63)	(.72)	(.66)	(.69)
	$n=14$	$n=13$	$n=12$	$n=14$	$n=13$	$n=13$

Note. Standard Deviations appear in parentheses.

Adapted from Berger, Knowlton and Abrahams (1996, Experiment 2). Reprinted with permission from Guilford Press.

words/second), $t(73) = 8.92$, $p < .001$. By contrast, during the second rendition of the directions, the average speech rates for these two groups were virtually identical ($M_{plan} = 2.48$ words/second; $M_{no\ plan} = 2.46$ words/second). In addition, those who planned showed a significant decrease in speech rate across renditions, $t(72) = 6.05$, $p < .001$, whereas those who did not plan showed a significant increase in speech rate from the first to the second rendition, $t(72) = 2.51$, $p < .02$.

As anticipated by the hypothesis, these results suggest that those who engaged in planning before their interactions initially were more verbally fluent than their counterparts who did not plan before they interacted. The results also indicate, however, that after receiving feedback from the confederates, there was little difference in the verbal fluency levels of the two groups during the second rendition of their directions. Furthermore, the initial fluency advantage that planners displayed during the first rendition of their directions dissipated by the second rendition, whereas those who did not plan in advance became more fluent during their second rendition.

In general, the results of this study lend further support to the hypothesis that higher level alterations to message-plan hierarchies place more demands on the cognitive system than do lower level modifications. Although preinteraction planning appears to facilitate verbal fluency initially, this effect seems to dissipate when a second rendition of the description is necessitated. In contrast to these findings, there was no support for the notion that preinteraction planning fixates direction givers on one route so that when they are asked for another route, cognitive demands are even larger. However, two important points should be kept in mind while evaluating these particular findings. First, exactly what participants thought about during the 3 minutes they were given to plan is not clear. For example, some participants may have spontaneously generated alternatives during this time, which, in turn, facilitated their performance when they were asked subsequently for an alternative route. Second, evidence reviewed in Chapter 3 clearly demonstrated support for a U-curve relationship between plan complexity and onset latency. Individuals with only one planned route and those with six alternative planned routes showed longer speech onset latencies when asked to provide a different route than those who planned only three alternative routes in advance. This same curve was found in a replication study employing a persuasion task (Knowlton, 1994). One plausible explanation for the degraded performance of those who prepared only one route or one argument in advance of presentation is the fixation notion outlined previously. Given the potential limitations of the planning manipulation used in the present experiment and the findings of the Knowlton (1994) studies, it is more than reasonable to invest additional research energy into the investigation of the fixation explanation.

Participants assigned to the Δ-Speech Rate condition in both this study and the previous experiment manifested speech onset latencies that, as predicted, were less than those obtained from participants assigned to conditions representing more abstract levels of message-plan hierarchies. It is the case that in both experiments, those in the Δ-Speech Rate condition showed no evidence of decreased speech rate when providing the second rendition of their directions; although, such decreases in speech rate across renditions were observed when language-based failures were manifested by Caucasian confederates in the first study of this series.

There are several alternative explanations for the failure of Δ-Speech Rate participants to reduce their speech rates, as would be expected. First, and potentially most troubling, participants may not have believed confederates when they said they had difficulty following the directions because the participant spoke too quickly. However, one significant difficulty with this explanation is that it begs the question of why the Δ-Route manipulation was believable and successful in both studies, and why the Δ-Landmarks induction was highly successful in the present experiment. Why should the Δ-Speech Rate induction be any less believable than the other two? A second, and theoretically more interesting possibility is that participants in the Δ-Speech Rate condition may have believed the confederates and thought that they actually did reduce their speech rate when providing the directions the second time. It is possible that speech rate, in relation to other speech parameters, is one that is particularly difficult for speakers to monitor and control. This explanation is especially appealing because the message-plan alterations requested of both Δ-Route and Δ-Landmarks participants were verbal in nature, whereas those requested of Δ-Speech Rate participants were nonverbal. Because it is commonly assumed that verbal behavior is more easily monitored and consciously controlled than nonverbal behavior (Knapp & Hall, 1992), this alternative explanation is worth some research attention.

Message Plan Hierarchy Levels and Cognitive Load: A Field Experiment. Although the preceding two studies presented compelling evidence to support the claim that abstract alterations to message plan hierarchies are more demanding cognitively than are lower level alterations, these studies were both conducted under several constraints in a laboratory situation. Before rendering their directions, participants were instructed not to ask the confederates any questions while providing the directions, and they were instructed to remain seated. This latter instruction was given because the videotaping was done with a stationary camera. Confederates were instructed not to answer any questions that participants might inadvertently ask. If participants requested more information regarding the confederates' failure to understand their directions, confederates were instructed simply to repeat what they had said previously. Given these constraints and the fact that the studies were conducted in a laboratory-like setting, a skeptic might argue that the findings are in some respects an artifact of the interaction constraints and the setting.

In order to allay these fears, a field experiment was conducted in which the Δ-Route, Δ-Landmarks, and Δ-Speech Rate inductions were enacted by experimenters in a public setting. Randomly selected pedestrians, who appeared to be of at least high-school age and who were walking alone, were approached by experimenter–observer pairs at the corner of a main intersection of a small college town. Experimenters asked directions either to the public library or to the university's stadium, both of which were some distance from the intersection. After pedestrians provided the first rendition of their directions, the experimenter enacted one of the three locus of communication failure inductions. Pedestrians were randomly assigned to one of these three inductions as well as to the destination condition. Each experimenter–observer team completed six interactions, one for each condition of the design. No teams were present at the intersection at the same time.

As observers stood silently by while these interactions transpired, they recorded two observations. First, using a concealed stop watch, they clocked the amount of time that lapsed between the point at which the experimenter ceased giving the communication failure induction and the point at which the pedestrian began the second rendition of his or her directions. Second, in addition to recording speech onset latency, observers noted whether pedestrians maintained or broke eye contact with the experimenter after receiving the locus of communication failure induction. This eye-gaze measure was incorporated into this study because some evidence suggests that when individuals are placed under high levels of cognitive load in social situations, they tend to avert eye gaze from interaction partners, presumably to reduce the level of stimulation from the environment (Day, 1964).

To determine whether destination made any difference in the cognitive load experienced by the participants, or whether destination might interact with the locus of communication failure, two 2 x 3 ANOVA's were computed using destination and locus of communication failure as independent variables, and onset latency and eye-gaze cessation as the dependent variables. The means and standard deviations for onset latency expressed in seconds are displayed in Table 4.4. Because the onset latency standard deviations increased with the means, a $\log_{10}$ transformation again was applied to homogenize the within-cell variances. These transformed scores were then submitted to variance analysis. The ANOVA revealed only a significant main effect for locus of communication failure, $F(2,78) = 5.17$, $p < .005$, $\eta^2 = .12$. The F values obtained for the destination main effect and the interaction were less than 1.00. Because the main hypothesis stipulated a directional relationship between locus of communication failure and onset latency, and because this experiment attempted to replicate a previously found relationship, planned contrasts (Winer, 1971) were used to compare

TABLE 4.4

Mean Speech Onset Latency in Seconds

	Locus of Communication Failure		
	Δ-Speech Rate	Δ-Landmarks	Δ-Route
Destination			
Stadium	2.51	5.02	6.57
	(1.75)	(5.48)	(6.92)
	n=14	n=14	n=14
Library	2.39	3.78	7.97
	(2.11)	(3.45)	(5.56)
	n=14	n=14	n=14
Total	2.45	4.40	7.27
	(1.90)	(4.54)	(6.21)
	n=28	n=28	n=28

Note. Standard deviations appear in parentheses.

the three locus of communication failure conditions. The Bartlett-Box test for homogeneity of variance of onset latencies among three locus of communication failure conditions was nonsignificant, $F = 1.02$, $p <.36$, indicating that the $\log_{10}$ transformation had the effect of homogenizing the variances. The planned contrasts revealed that the mean onset latency for the Δ-Landmarks condition was significantly greater than the mean for the Δ-Speech Rate condition, $t(81) = 1.91$, $p <.05$. The mean onset latency for the Δ-Route condition was also significantly greater than the mean for the Δ-Speech Rate condition, $t(81) = 3.39$, $p <.005$. Finally, although the mean for the Δ-Route condition was greater than the mean for the Δ-Landmarks condition as predicted, this difference fell short of conventional significance levels, $t(81) = 1.47$, $p <.10$. Nevertheless, the pattern of the onset latency means replicated the one observed in the previous two studies.

Although the transformed onset latency measure and the eye gaze aversion index were positively related ($r = .20$), this correlation was not significant. Consequently, the eye-gaze index of cognitive load was analyzed separately. While this variable was scored dichotomously, with the higher number indicating a break in eye-gaze, the distributions on the variable were such that it could be analyzed using conventional ANOVA procedures (D'Agostino, 1971). The means and standard deviations for the eye-gaze index are shown in Table 4.5. Although the pattern of means displayed in Table 4.5 is consistent with theoretical expectations, the ANOVA of these data produced no significant main effects or a significant interaction effect. All of the F values were less than 1.00. Of the 84 people who participated in the experiment, 73% broke eye gaze with the confederate immediately after receiving their feedback. The percentage of participants in each locus of communication failure condition who broke eye gaze was 71%, 68%, and 82% for the Δ-Speech Rate, Δ-Landmarks, and the Δ-Route conditions, respectively. These relatively high rates of eye gaze aversion across all conditions suggest the possibility that a ceiling effect on this index may have prevented a reasonable assessment of this hypothesis.

The findings of this field experiment should put to rest any qualms concerning the internal validity of the laboratory studies demonstrating increased cognitive load when individuals alter message plan hierarchies at higher levels of abstraction. Moreover, the effect size associated with this significant relationship in the noisy field environment of the present study was of similar magnitude to the one obtained in the less noisy laboratory setting ($\eta^2 = .12$ vs. $\eta^2 = .16$); although, in the other laboratory study a more robust effect size of $\eta^2 = .33$ was obtained. Furthermore, the fact that the same pattern of speech onset latency differences among the locus of communication failure conditions was observed regardless of destination manipulation, and the fact that the study was conducted on a randomly selected group of pedestrians, rather than the usual volunteer samples of college undergraduates such as those used in the previous studies in this series, should increase confidence in the external validity of this effect.

The failure of the eye-gaze aversion measure to reflect the differences detected by the speech onset latency measure is subject to multiple explanations. First, as already suggested, the rates of gaze aversion across all

Table 4.5

Mean Eye-Gaze Aversion

	Locus of Communication Failure		
	Δ-Speech Rate	Δ-Landmarks	Δ-Route
Destination			
Stadium	1.71	1.71	1.86
	(.47)	(.47)	(.36)
	$n = 14$	$n = 14$	$n = 14$
Library	1.71	1.64	1.79
	(.47)	(.50)	(.43)
	$n = 14$	$n = 14$	$n = 14$
Total	1.71	1.68	1.79
	(.47)	(.48)	(.39)
	$n = 28$	$n = 28$	$n = 28$

Note. Higher score indicates eye gaze aversion. Standard deviations appear in parentheses.

conditions were relatively high, thus setting up the possibility that potential variations among conditions could not manifest themselves. A second, and closely related explanation, is that while eye-gaze aversion may be an indicant of increased cognitive load, aversion may occur at relatively low thresholds of cognitive load and thus remain insensitive to changes in cognitive load at higher levels. By contrast, speech onset latency may be a more sensitive indicator of cognitive load across the entire spectrum of its variation. Finally, a less theoretically interesting but nonetheless plausible possibility, concerns the reliability of measurement of eye-gaze aversion. Given the design of this study, it was not possible to estimate the reliability with which observers recorded either eye gaze aversion or speech onset latency. Whereas the onset latency data comport well with data obtained in the laboratory studies, on which reliability checks were performed with very positive results, we have no idea of how reliable the eye-gaze data are. Consequently, it is possible that unreliability of measurement prevented significant effects from emerging in the analysis.

Message Plan Hierarchy Levels and Cognitive Load: A Field Replication. A second field experiment was conducted that replicated the Δ-Speech Rate and Δ-Route conditions of the previous field experiment in the same location (Berger et al., 1996, Experiment 4). In this study, destination was held constant and the number of individuals showing lack of understanding was varied to see whether this factor would act to increase cognitive load, especially among those in the Δ-Route condition. Specifically, it was reasoned that having more than one person show lack of understanding to a direction giver would induce the giver to entertain more alternative possibilities before delivering the second rendition of the directions, thus increasing cognitive load. However, this additional indication of lack of understanding should not have an effect on cognitive load within the Δ-Speech Rate condition because the message plan alteration being asked for by multiple parties is the same, that is, a reduction in speech rate during the second rendition of the directions.

Again, experimenter–observer pairs randomly selected solo pedestrians who appeared to be of at least high school age to participate in the experiment. The pedestrians were approached at the same intersection and asked for directions to the university stadium. After providing the first rendition of the directions, the experimenter gave one of the two locus of communication failure inductions. While the experimenter delivered this induction, the observer did one of two things. In the Experimenter Only condition, the observer stood quietly to the side while the experimenter spoke to the direction giver, as observers had done in the previous field experiment. In the Experimenter–Observer condition, the observers nodded their assent as the experimenters delivered the induction. Observers did not speak, but they made it obvious that they agreed with the experimenter. Observers unobtrusively recorded speech onset latency and eye-gaze aversion as they did in the previous experiment. Each experimenter–observer team completed one interaction for each of the four experimental conditions of the design.

To determine the independent and conjoint effects of locus of communication failure and pervasiveness of communication failure on cognitive load, two 2 x 2 ANOVA's were computed employing onset latency and eye-gaze aversion as dependent variables. The means and standard deviations for onset latency expressed in seconds are displayed in Table 4.6. Again, speech onset latencies were transformed ($\log_{10}$). The ANOVA of the transformed onset latency measure produced no significant main effects or a significant interaction; however, the main effect for the locus of communication failure approached significant levels, $F(1,64) = 2.25$, $p < .14$. As the data displayed in Table 4.6 show, individuals who were asked to provide a new route in the second rendition of their directions (Δ-Route) took more time ($M = 7.45s$) to begin giving their directions than did their counterparts who were asked to give their directions a second time but at a slower speech rate (Δ-Speech, $M = 4.01s$). The other main effect and the interaction effect were not significant.

Because considerable variance among the within cell variances remained after applying the $\log_{10}$ transformation, a nonparametric, Mann-Whitney U test was computed which contrasted the onset latency scores between the Δ-Speech and Δ-Route conditions. This analysis produced a significant outcome, $Z = 1.96$, $p < .025$. The results of this analysis again lend support to the hierarchical levels–cognitive load relationship; however, although the pattern of means displayed in Table 4.6 is consistent with the interaction hypothesis, that is, larger onset latency differences between the pervasiveness of failure conditions within the Δ-Route condition than within the

TABLE 4.6

Speech Onset Latency in Seconds

| | Locus of Communication Failure | |
	Δ-Speech Rate	Δ-Route
Failure Pervasiveness		
Experimenter Only	M=3.88	M=6.42
	(3.28)	(6.10)
	n=18	n=18
Experimenter-Confederate	M=4.15	M=8.47
	(3.30)	(9.08)
	n=18	n=18

Note. Standard deviations appear in parentheses.

Δ-Speech Rate condition, this interaction failed to reach conventional significance levels.

Although the onset latency measure and the eye gaze aversion index were positively related ($r = .16$), this correlation was not significant. Consequently, the eye-gaze index of cognitive load was again analyzed separately. This variable again was scored dichotomously, with the higher number indicating a break in eye-gaze. The distributions on the variable were such that it could be analyzed using conventional ANOVA procedures (D'Agostino, 1971). The means and standard deviations for the eye gaze index are shown in Table 4.7. Of the 72 pedestrians who participated in the study, 53 (73.60%) averted their eye-gaze before giving the second rendition of their directions. The ANOVA of the eye-gaze aversion data produced no significant main effects. Thus, eye-gaze aversion did not increase when higher level message-plan alterations were requested; moreover, the interaction between locus of communication failure and pervasiveness of communication failure also was nonsignificant.

The results of this experiment suggest at least two conclusions. First, the association between locus of communication failure and speech onset latency was replicated in a field setting, thus adding further confidence to the veracity of this relationship. It should be noted that across the four experiments in this series, including the present one, no significant speech onset latency differences were found between males and females. Apparently, the relationship suggested by the Hierarchy Principle is not conditioned by gender differences. Second, the eye-gaze aversion measure neither correlated well with the speech onset latency index nor showed a significant relationship with locus of communication failure. Potential explanations for the failure of this variable to comport well with the speech onset latency

TABLE 4.7

Eye Gaze Aversion

	Locus of Communication Failure	
	Δ-Speech Rate	Δ-Route
Failure Pervasiveness		
Experimenter Only	M = 1.67	M = 1.72
	(.49)	(.46)
	n = 18	n = 18
Experimenter-Confederate	M = 1.78	M = 1.78
	(.43)	(.43)
	n = 18	n = 18

Note: Larger numbers indicate higher proportions of gaze aversion.

measure already have been considered. Until more data can be gathered to assess the reliability of measurement of this variable, it would not seem wise to continue to use it as a potential measure of cognitive load.

SUMMARY

Consistent with the Hierarchy Principle, strategic communicators who are thwarted in reaching their goals display a distinct propensity to alter message-plan hierarchies at relatively low levels of abstraction. These tendencies manifested themselves in experiments in which communicators demonstrated a proclivity to alter such low-level message-plan attributes as vocal intensity and speech rate in the face of communication failure, and to avoid higher level alterations to message content and sequencing. It was argued that this bias in favor of low-level changes arises because modifications at higher levels of message-plan hierarchies are cognitively more demanding and that individuals tend to be "cognitive misers." The first of these two postulates was tested directly in a series of two laboratory and two field experiments in which individuals were asked to make message plan modifications at various hierarchical levels in response to communication failure. Using speech onset latency as an index of cognitive load, across all four experiments significant increases in cognitive load were associated with higher level message-plan hierarchy alterations, thus leading to the conclusion that higher level message-plan alterations indeed are more cognitively demanding than are lower level modifications.

Chapter 5

Plan Effectiveness and Communicative Performance

80 ◆ og

To this point, the issue of plan effectiveness has been addressed only tangentially. In discussing plan effectiveness, it is useful to recall the distinction made in chapter 2 between plans and planning. Effective social plans are those that enable people to reach primary goals while satisfying the metagoals of efficiency and social appropriateness. Effective planning is a cognitive process that produces effective plans. Although these definitions are relatively straightforward, they belie the fact that in practice, assessing the effectiveness of both plans and planning is quite difficult.

The effectiveness of any action plan aimed at achieving a social goal is the joint product of the plan, and the skills and attributes of the social actor who carries out the plan. For example, a person could develop a very sophisticated and potentially effective plan to change another person's opinion on an issue; however, because the planner has an odd vocal pitch, a speech impediment, or an abrasive interaction style, the plan might fail to bring about the desired outcome. Experience tells us that there are individuals who are excellent planners in particular social domains but who cannot enact their superior plans with the requisite skill to bring about the desired result. Also, there are people who have very effective communication styles who are themselves not very apt planners. This is why politicians have speech writers. Speech writers are planning specialists, whereas politicians presumably have the communication skills necessary to realize these plans in action. Speech writers may not themselves be able to present an effective speech; just as politicians may not be able to plan one. Table 5.1 displays the potential joint impact of plan effectiveness and communication skills and attributes on the ultimate effectiveness of plans.

As Table 5.1 indicates, there is a higher probability that a social goal will be achieved when the plan itself is effective and the planner has the requisite communication attributes and skills. The probability of goal attainment is

TABLE 5.1

Plan Effectiveness, Performative Skill and Goal Attainment

	Plan Effectiveness	
	Low	*High*
Performative Skill		
Low	Low Probability of Goal Attainment	Moderate Probability of Goal Attainment
High	Moderate Probability of Goal Attainment ("Style" but no "substance.")	High Probability of Goal Attainment

reduced when a plan is relatively ineffective and communication attributes and skills are negative. The two intermediate cases are likely to fall somewhere between these extremes in terms of the likelihood of goal attainment and, as Table 5.1 indicates, highly effective plans that are poorly realized because of negative communication attributes and skills are likely to be judged to have considerable substance but no "style." By contrast, plans that themselves are relatively low in effectiveness, but enacted with a high level of performative acumen are likely to give rise to such judgments as "style but no substance." Because the focus of the present effort is on plans and planning, the contribution of performance skills to effectiveness is not considered further; nevertheless, it is obvious that stylistic aspects of communication are related to the effectiveness with which social goals are attained. The focus now shifts to the issues of plan and planning effectiveness. Some alternative approaches to the assessment of plan effectiveness are considered. Then, some alternative ways of viewing planning effectiveness are outlined.

ASSESSING PLAN EFFECTIVENESS

A Priori Approaches

One potential method for assessing the effectiveness of a plan is to have individuals create plans to achieve goals and then have the plans evaluated before any attempt is made to reach the goal. In this case the assessment of plan effectiveness is independent of whether the plan actually brings about the desired end state. For example, one might ask two young teenage boys each to devise a plan for asking a girl out for a date. One of the boys might simply say that he would approach the girl and ask her out. The other might concoct an elaborate plan involving such actions as asking third parties, who are familiar with the prospective date, for information about her current dating status (Is she already attached to someone?), musical preferences (Does she like punk or heavy metal?), movie preferences (Does she like horror movies?), and other potentially relevant information. The more elaborate plan might also include asking third parties to find out whether a date request would be accepted if offered.

Intuitively, it is tempting to conclude that because the second planner developed a considerably more complex plan than the first, the second planner's plan is the more effective one. The problem with this conclusion is that it is possible that in a particular circumstance, the simple, more direct plan might be more effective. For instance, working through third parties might be perceived by the prospective date as a sign of excessive shyness on the part of the second planner. If the prospective date was not attracted to excessively shy boys, this fact might undermine the ultimate effectiveness of the second planner's plan. In addition, if the prospective date were already attracted to the date requester, the simple plan might be all that is necessary.

Consistent with the previous discussion of plan complexity and action fluidity, it might be argued that, in general, complex plans are more likely to be effective than are simple ones, especially when thwarting takes place. Complex plans are more likely than simple ones to contain action contingencies that enable social actors to circumvent goal blocks. Nonetheless, it is possible that even a complex plan will not contain the optimal path to a goal; whereas a simple plan might contain few or no contingencies but represent the optimal action sequence that is not subject to blockage because of its overwhelming effectiveness.

Beyond the issue of plan complexity and effectiveness, it is reasonable to suppose that people might be able to make quite reliable judgments of the potential debilitating effects of socially undesirable actions in social plans. For example, in devising a plan to persuade a job interviewer that one should be hired, the interviewee who includes actions that represent threats and intimidation might be judged confidently to have developed a plan that is very likely to be ineffective in almost any imaginable job interview context, except perhaps for becoming a pugilist. In contrast to the ease with which extremely socially inappropriate actions might be judged to undermine the potential effectiveness of plans, judging the potential effectiveness or ineffectiveness of socially desirable actions presents more of a problem. For instance, as part of a plan to ingratiate one self to another, one might explicitly say that one would smile often to enhance his or her attractiveness. The difficulty in this instance is that in practice, the person might smile too much and appear to be obsequious, thus potentially lowering his or her attractiveness.

The relatively unambiguous negative effects of socially undesirable actions and the relatively ambiguous effects of socially desirable actions is most likely a reflection of the effects of assumed desirability of actions on their diagnostic value. In their correspondent inference theory, Jones and Davis (1965) claimed that when individuals behave in socially undesirable ways or out of role, observers are more likely to judge their actions to be representative of underlying personality dispositions. Thus, when a person shows anger in a social context where displays of anger are ordinarily constrained, observers are likely to assume that the angry person has an angry disposition. By contrast, when individuals produce actions congruent with role expectations or actions that have a high level of social desirability, it becomes more difficult to confidently draw a link between observed actions and underlying dispositions. People may be extremely friendly for a wide variety of reasons other than the fact that they have a friendly disposition. The theoretical relationships described in correspondent inference theory obviously apply to the problem of making a priori effectiveness judgments of planned actions.

To this point the idea of a priori assessment of plan effectiveness has been discussed as if it were a unitary concept. Actually, there are at least two different varieties of a priori effectiveness assessment. The first type involves the application of a set of criteria to a plan to determine the extent to which the plan conforms to an a priori conception of effectiveness. The criteria used to make these judgments would follow from a theory of plan effectiveness. The second type of a priori assessment would be considerably less rigorous and would involve the subjective judgments of groups of individuals. In this case, judges would be asked to read plans and indicate the degree to which the plan would be effective if it were to be enacted. Of course, the degree to which judges are provided with criteria for evaluating plans could be varied.

It is worth reiterating here that very precise a priori estimates of at least some aspects of plan effectiveness can be made when some types of nonsocial goals are pursued. Studies that ask people to plan a sequence of errands, when given a map of a town (Hayes-Roth & Hayes-Roth, 1979), or plan a series of chores in a classroom, given a diagram of the room (Pea & Hawkins, 1987), can reveal the extent to which the planned route developed by a given study participant has deviated from some optimal path. That is, such planning tasks can be structured so that there is one and only one route that takes the least amount of time and effort to execute. However, in planning to reach social goals, the notion of an optimal action sequence is considerably more murky; moreover, in planning for social goals, one must contend with a moving target and a dynamic set of circumstances. Maps of towns and diagrams of classrooms generally do not change in the course of planning activities. By contrast, as planners think about what they might do to attain social goals, their planning may be influenced by the dynamic properties of the imagined interaction situation. Consequently, defining a single, optimal course of action for reaching a particular social goal as a way of generating criteria for assessing plan effectiveness would seem to be extremely difficult, if not impossible.

A Posteriori Assessment

Another approach to determining the effectiveness of plans is to carry out the plan and see whether the goal or goals desired by the planner are achieved. Under this view, effective plans are those that generate courses of action that produce desired end states, and ineffective plans are those that generate action sequences that fail to result in the attainment of desired goals. Although this view has a great deal of intuitive and practical appeal, its adequacy may be at least somewhat illusory for a number of reasons. First, attainment of a goal or a set of goals by following a planned course of action does not certify, ipso facto, that it was the course of action that was responsible for producing the desired end state. For example, one might develop a plan to ingratiate one self to another person that is based on the idea that doing favors for others is likely to induce the desired liking (Jones, 1964; Jones & Wortman, 1973). Assuming this course of action is followed and the target of the ingratiation plan becomes more attracted to the ingratiator, it is possible that the increase in attraction had little or nothing to do with the fact that the ingratiator did favors for the target. The target may be attracted to the ingratiator because the ingratiator smiled frequently or displayed a friendly interaction style, variables not included in the ingratiator's original plan. The goal indeed was attained, but not because of the actions generated directly by the ingratiator's plan.

A second problem with employing goal attainment as a criterion for judging plan effectiveness involves the flip side of the first problem. Plans that fail to bring about desired end states may be effective but fail for extraordinary reasons. These extraordinary reasons may involve external sources of goal blockage for which it might be difficult if not impossible to plan. Assume, for example, that a person has devised a potentially very effective plan to persuade another to change his opinion on an issue. Our hypothetical planner is in the midst of executing the plan during an interaction with the target when a severe earthquake hits, making it impossible for the planner to complete the plan and attain the persuasion objective. The goal has not been achieved, but not because the plan itself necessarily was ineffective.

Third, a somewhat less extreme case than the one just considered concerns the proportion of times a particular action plan works when it is deployed. This case is somewhat different from the first two in that the focus of the first two cases was on an individual event, whereas the present case focuses on the statistical aggregate of events. What if the same plan is used on repeated occasions and is successful in producing the desired outcome 80% of the time. Is this an effective plan? It is difficult to answer this question in any absolute sense. Perhaps the most reasonable answer is: "It depends." What "it" depends on is a judgment relative to some criterion or to some other plan. Thus, if the 80% effective plan in question is one designed to sell a product over the telephone, an 80% success rate might be very effective, given the costs necessary to develop and implement the plan. Or, compared with another telephone solicitation plan with a success rate of 40%, the 80% success rate plan might look quite good. Of course, 80% is not 100% and there may be the desire to increase the effectiveness of the 80% effective plan. Here, other considerations may become salient; for example, the costs of developing a still more effective plan versus the amount of additional effectiveness that might be gained through such efforts.

Finally, it was pointed out previously that attaining any social goal is the joint product of the quality of a plan and the degree to which the planner has the communication skills necessary to realize the plan in action. Given this distinction, it is clear that individuals may fail to reach social goals not because of defective plans but because they lack the communication skills necessary to do so. Because an effective plan is necessary but not sufficient for goal attainment, failure to reach a goal cannot be linked unambiguously with lack of plan effectiveness.

The four problems raised here suggest that the a posteriori assessment of plan effectiveness is considerably more complex than might be supposed. Simply because people are successful in reaching social goals does not mean that they were following an effective plan; and failure to reach a social goal does not necessarily mean that an inferior plan was being followed. These conceptual possibilities raise obvious challenges to the a posteriori assessment of plan effectiveness.

Assessing Planning Effectiveness

Planning effectiveness concerns the extent to which individuals employ procedures that produce effective plans. A number of approaches to effective planning have been suggested by researchers from a wide variety of disciplines. For example, strategic planning is an important topic in management science as well as in urban planning (Holloway, 1986; Sillince, 1986). Those working in these areas almost universally extol the virtues of planning and suggest different approaches to effective planning. Holloway (1986) argued for the necessity of setting organizational objectives and more specific goals, developing programs or plans to reach these goals, implementing programs, and modifying plans as feedback is received. He also discussed the importance of considering the time horizon within which one is planning. Plans that are projected over very long time periods may be rendered useless because of changes that occur in the environment during the period for which the planning was done.

Sillince (1986) distinguished between the rational–comprehensive approach to urban planning and the disjointed–incrementalist strategy. Using the rational–comprehensive approach, the planner defines goals, arranges goals into subgoals, generates a complete array of alternative solutions, evaluates these alternatives, and implements the preferred alternative. By contrast, under the disjointed–incrementalism approach, choice is made only at the margin, there are only a small number of alternatives, a small number of consequences is calculated, goals are adjusted to what is feasible, information is seen as value-laden, problems are only alleviated, not solved, and there are many decision makers. Sillince (1986) contended that because urban planning frequently is carried out in a politically–charged environ-ment, disjointed–incrementalism is considerably more likely to be used than is the rational–comprehensive approach. He avers that disjointed incremen-talism might be superior to the rational–comprehensive approach within the urban planning domain.

In chapter 2 the distinction was made between top–down and bottom–up planning. It was pointed out that individuals most likely employ both of these planning modes when devising plans to reach social goals. Also, they may develop only partial plans that are filled in as the plan is executed (Bratman, 1987, 1990). It would be difficult to argue for the superiority of one of these alternatives over the other without considering a number of variables. By taking into account certain attributes of the social situation and the target of goal-directed action, it might be possible to argue convinc-ingly for the potential effectiveness of one of these approaches over the other given certain circumstances. For example, when one is attempting to attain social goals with a target who is known well, and in a situation where the likelihood of environmental perturbations is low, a top–down planning strategy might be most appropriate, because relatively less attention needs to be paid to the appearance of plan-thwarting events. By contrast, when the target is not well known and the environment contains the potential for many possible thwarting events, planning may have to be based more on events as they unfold during the interaction; that is, planning may have to be done "on the fly."

Another way to think about these relationships is in terms of uncertainty. When uncertainty about the target person and the environment is relatively low, then top-down planning that produces considerable detail is possible and probably desirable. However, when uncertainty is relatively high, it might be futile to develop plans at the abstract level and deduce specific actions from these broader categories. In these high-uncertainty situations, instead of engaging in extensive planning, time might be better spent gathering information about the person and the environment in order to formulate potentially effective plans. Consequently, an effective plan for dealing with highly uncertain situations would most likely include a sub plan for information gathering, as a prerequisite to the action planning necessary to guide conduct toward desired goals.

As was the case with assessing plan effectiveness, the determination of planning effectiveness is fraught with difficulties. For example, assume that one of the planning approaches just outlined is followed, and an effective plan is produced. Suppose further that the plan is effective in both a priori and a posteriori senses. Can it be asserted unequivocally that the planning process that produced the effective plan was itself effective? The answer to this question is clearly "no." As noted previously, goals may be attained for reasons that have little or nothing to do with the effectiveness of the plan itself. If a plan is effective, it cannot be assumed that the process that produced the plan was also effective. On the other side of the coin, a similar problem arises when a plan fails. As noted earlier, plans may fail for extraordinary reasons not related to their intrinsic effectiveness; as a result, concluding that a failed plan was the product of a flawed planning process may be unwarranted.

The lesson to be gleaned from this discussion of planning effectiveness is that there is no flaw-free method for indexing the effectiveness of planning, especially at the level of the single case; however, before being overwhelmed with pessimism, there would seem to be at least a partial solution to these problems. One might be more confident about inferences concerning planning effectiveness if repeated applications of the same planning routine were consistently to produce plans with a particular level of effectiveness. Moreover, using the same plan to reach the same goal across a wide variety of circumstances might provide some indication of the plan's effectiveness, assuming that the outcomes across the various situations were similar. Successful replications might warrant increased confidence in our inferences concerning planning effectiveness.

PLAN EFFECTIVENESS AND SOCIAL COMPETENCE

Although there has been no research reported concerning relationships between planning effectiveness and social competence, there have been studies that have found links between plan effectiveness and social competence (Berger & Bell, 1988; Berger & diBattista, 1992a). In addition, relationships between plan effectiveness and cognitive abilities have been examined in at least one study (Jordan, 1993). Others have assessed the degree to which initial planning (Battman, 1989) and repeated planning opportunities influence the optimality of planned actions (Pea & Hawkins, 1987). Although this research has not involved social goals directly, it will be reviewed presently because of its potential heuristic value for the study of plan effectiveness in the social domain.

Initial Planning and Plan Efficacy

In a study designed to determine whether the opportunity to plan would produce more efficient goal-directed action, Battman (1989) contrasted the performance of those who planned before participating in a simulated traveling salesman game with those who did not plan before engaging in the same simulation. This study revealed that planning before participating in the simulation improved the efficiency of the route taken by the hypothetical salesman. Planners were more likely than nonplanners to reschedule appointment times, indicating that they had analyzed the problem and generated plans that focused on rearranging the sequence of scheduled stops. Although this study demonstrates that planning can improve efficiency, it does not indicate the mechanisms responsible for the increased efficiency.

Replanning and Plan Efficacy

The general question addressed here concerns the degree to which individuals improve the efficiency of their plans when they are given opportunities to revise plans. This idea was tested directly in a study by Pea and Hawkins (1987). Children ranging in age from 8 to12 years were given the task of planning the order in which they would do such classroom chores as cleaning blackboards, arranging chairs around a table, feeding a hamster, and so on. The locations in which these tasks were to be performed were represented on a diagram of the classroom. As they observed the classroom map, children were asked to devise a plan which would define the *shortest way* of accomplishing all of the chores. They were told that the shortest way would be the *best way*. After completing their first plans, the children were asked if they could make up a shorter plan for accomplishing the tasks. Children who answered this query in the affirmative were given the opportunity to develop another plan. The experimental session ended when children believed they had arrived at the shortest possible plan for accomplishing the tasks.

Comparisons between initial and subsequent plans revealed that subsequent plans generally were more efficient than were initial plans. This finding led Pea and Hawkins (1987) to conclude that good planners appear to engage in cycles of plan revision and simulation to develop and test increasingly efficient plan organizations. Furthermore, based on analyses of the hierarchical levels at which plan revisions were made, these researchers observed:

> Certainly our planning results indicate how rarely children engaged in revisions in which they 'stepped back' and redefined the planning situation after beginning to construct a plan. The finding that high-level decision-making decreased from first to last plan among children further suggests that children's planning efforts consisted of refining an initial conception, rather than considering top-level reorganization of the plan. (Pea & Hawkins, 1987, p. 297)

These preferences for low-level rather than high-level plan alterations are consistent with both the pattern of plan modifications predicted by the hierarchy principle discussed in chapters 2 and 4 and the findings of the studies corroborating this principle that were described in detail in chapter 4.

Although the findings of this study suggest that individuals indeed may be able to fashion progressively more efficient plans when given the opportunity to reevaluate old plans, it should be kept in mind that participants in this study were very explicitly told that the shortest plan would be the best one. Thus, participants were provided with a clear planning goal toward which they might strive. In many everyday planning situations, including some of those that do not involve social goals, such criteria may not be as explicit and clear to planners as they were in this study. Consequently, under these less well-defined conditions, repeated planning might not produce increments in the efficiency of plans.

Plan Effectiveness and Social Loneliness

In the previous experiment, because of the nature of the task, plan efficiency could be determined with reference to an obvious standard; however, as was noted earlier, when social goals are pursued, such clear-cut criteria generally are unavailable for assessing plan effectiveness. Consequently, other approaches to determining plan effectiveness must be employed when social goals are the objects of study. Two studies exploring the relationships between plan effectiveness and social loneliness exemplify such an alternative approach (Berger & Bell, 1988; Berger & diBattista, 1992a).

In both of these studies, each research participant was asked to write two different plans, one for achieving the goal of asking someone out for a date (Date-Request) and one for inducing a new roommate to like oneself (Roommate Ingratiation). Under the guise of participating in separate study, participants were asked to complete a number of measures including the revised version of the UCLA Loneliness Scale (Russell, 1982; Russell, Peplau, & Cutrona, 1980). Plans written by research participants were typed on separate sheets of paper and given to panels of judges, balanced with respect to gender. Judges were asked to sort the plans on an 11-point effectiveness continuum ranging from "extremely ineffective" to "extremely effective." Judges were not told what constituted an effective plan; they were simply told to read each plan and to estimate the degree to which they thought the plan would be effective, if it were carried out. Separate panels of judges sorted the two different types of plans. Estimates of interjudge agreement for the plan effectiveness judgments in both of these studies were in the .70 to .85 range.

In both of these studies no significant correlations were found between the effectiveness judgments for both of these goals, indicating that effective planners in one of these domains were not necessarily effective planners in the other domain. Because previous research in the population used in these studies indicated that males asked females out for dates significantly more frequently than females asked out males, it was reasoned that plan effectiveness in the date-request domain would be correlated inversely with social loneliness for males but not for females. The reasoning underlying this prediction was that because males generally initiate requests for dates with females, their effectiveness in this domain should have significantly more impact on their levels of felt loneliness than would be the case for females who tend not to initiate date requests. By contrast, because both males and females may pursue the goal of inducing a roommate to like them, there should be inverse correlations of about equal magnitudes between plan effectiveness in this domain and social loneliness for members of both sexes. Table 5.2 displays the relevant data from both studies regarding these predicted relationships.

As the data of Table 5.2 show, the pattern of correlations predicted here is most evident in Berger and Bell's (1988) study and is partially replicated by Berger and diBattista's (1992a) investigation. Apparently, within the date-request domain, males with more effective plans are less lonely than males whose date-request plans are judged ineffective, whereas for females, for whom requesting dates is not a salient activity, there is no significant relationship between plan effectiveness and social loneliness. By contrast, in general there are inverse relationships between plan effectiveness and social loneliness for both males and females within the roommate ingratiation domain; although, this relationship was not significant for males in the Berger and diBattista (1992a) study.

A third study, which included the date-request scenario and the UCLA Loneliness Scale, showed a pattern of differences between males and females with respect to the correlation between social loneliness and plan effectiveness similar to that observed in the previous two studies (Jordan, 1993). In this investigation, social loneliness and plan effectiveness were correlated negatively ($r = -.20$) for males ($n = 9$), whereas among females ($n = 23$) the correlation was virtually zero ($r = .05$). Unfortunately, the power of this study's design was so low that the correlation among males failed to reach

TABLE 5.2

Correlations Between Plan Effectiveness and Loneliness by Goal and Gender

	Berger & Bell (1988)	Berger & diBattista (1992a)
	r	r
Goal and Sex		
Date-Request-Males	−.37**	−.34
Date-Request-Females	−.03	.06
Roommate-Ingratiation-Males	−.24*	.12
Roommate Ingratiation-Females	−.38***	−.40*

*$p < .05$; **$p < .01$; ***$p < .001$

Table adapted from Berger & Bell (1988) and Berger & diBattista (1992a). Reprinted with permission from Sage Publications.

significant levels; nevertheless, the pattern of difference matches that obtained in the other two studies.

There are at least three issues that must be considered concerning these findings. First, because these data are correlational, it is difficult to argue for the causal direction of the significant relationships. Consequently, at this point it is just as plausible to argue that it is not plan ineffectiveness that causes social loneliness, but that individuals who are particularly socially lonely have difficulty generating effective plans for reaching the kinds of social goals employed in these studies. This line of argument suggests that lonely individuals tend to lack the experience necessary to formulate effective plans for reaching social goals. Another alternative would be to postulate some kind of reciprocal causal relationship between plan effectiveness and social loneliness. Under this view, lonely individuals not only lack the requisite knowledge for formulating effective plans, but when they attempt to achieve social goals, they tend to experience higher rates of failure because their plans are relatively ineffective. These repeated goal failures contribute, in turn, to increased feelings of loneliness. In all likelihood, the kind of negative spiral implied by this reciprocal causal hypothesis comes closer to capturing the dynamics of this process than does any simple, recursive causal model.

A second issue left open by these studies concerns the plan effectiveness judgments themselves. Although the panels of judges employed in these three studies were able to make reliable effectiveness judgments, in the sense implied by interjudge agreement, and these judgments generally correlated with social loneliness as predicted, these findings leave open the question of what specific cues judges used to judge the relative effectiveness of the plans. Berger and Bell (1988) reported that date-request and roommate-ingratiation plans that were judged to be more effective were significantly longer and contained a greater variety of action units than plans judged to be less effective (r's ranged from .32 to .50). This study also revealed that date-request plans in which planners explicitly stated that they would seek to discover similarities between their potential dating partner and themselves as a way of asking their potential partner out were judged to be significantly more effective than plans not containing this action ($r = .33$). Roommate ingratiation plans containing the following actions were judged to be more effective: engage in a social activity with the new roommate in a setting outside of the room ($r = .34$), establish rules for living together ($r = .27$); and present a positive image to the new roommate ($r = .25$). More work needs to be done to tease out additional determinants of judged effectiveness. Given that judged plan effectiveness is related consistently to such measures as social loneliness, understanding in detail the determinants of judged plan effectiveness could provide valuable clues to the specific processes responsible for producing the general relationship between these two variables.

A third question, related to the first but not addressed directly by these findings, asks about the factors responsible for the relationships between plan effectiveness and social loneliness across both of the goals employed in these studies. Ancillary data reported by Berger and Jordan (1991) provide some beginning answers to this question. In this study, participants each were asked to devise plans for reaching four different goals, including the date-request and roommate-ingratiation goals. These plans were rendered within the context of a think-aloud task with retrospective reports (Ericsson & Simon, 1984). After verbalizing each plan, participants were asked to indicate what they were thinking as they provided the plan. These follow-up responses were analyzed for knowledge sources that individuals used to generate their plans (Berger & Jordan, 1992). On completing the think-aloud task, participants were asked to rank the four goals in terms of how difficult it was for them to devise a plan for that goal. Under the guise of participating in another experiment, participants also completed a questionnaire that included the revised UCLA loneliness scale.

Although the plans generated by the participants in this investigation were not judged for their effectiveness, rank order correlations (r_s) revealed that for males, loneliness was positively related to the ranked difficulty of the date-request goal ($r_s = .38, p < .02$). The same correlation for females was non-significant ($r_s = .19$). Thus, lonely males tended to find the date-request goal significantly more difficult to plan for than did their male counterparts with lower loneliness levels. In addition, males with higher levels of loneliness were significantly less likely to mention prior specific date-request episodes as a knowledge source for their present date-request plans ($r_s = -.32, p < .05$). Within the roommate ingratiation domain, lonely males were more likely to indicate spontaneously that they would not bother to try to induce their new roommate to like them ($r_s = -.27, p < .08$). By contrast, lonely females were more likely to say that they would not know how to ingratiate themselves to a new roommate ($r_s = .26, p < .05$).

Additional data from two studies are consistent with the findings of this investigation. Berger and Bell (1988) reported significant positive correlations between class rank and plan effectiveness in the date-request domain for both males ($r = .41, p < .001$) and females ($r = .39, p < .001$); however, no significant relationships between roommate ingratiation plan effectiveness and class rank were observed for either gender. One would expect plan effectiveness to increase with experience, especially in domains where the opportunity for repeated enactment of plans presents itself frequently. Because the production and reception of date requests are probably more frequent events in the lives of most college students than are initial encounters with new roommates, the accretion of date-request and date-request reception experience over the course of a college career is associated with the generation of more effective date-request plans.

The contrast between the significant positive correlations between date-request plan effectiveness and class rank for *both* males and females, and the *differential* correlations between date-request plan effectiveness and social loneliness for males and females could be suggestive of some kind of theoretical inconsistency. However, it is possible to explain these differential correlations. Simply put, both males and females may increase their date-request plan effectiveness over time by experiencing either being asked for a date or asking someone for a date. However, when it comes to feelings of social loneliness, the consequences of varying levels of date-request plan effectiveness are only experienced by those who actually request dates. Within the populations included in these studies, this task falls dispropor-tionately on males. Consequently, among males, date-request plan effective-ness is associated with feelings of social loneliness, whereas among females differences in date-request plan effectiveness are irrelevant at the level of social action. Consequently, differential plan effectiveness in this domain has little impact on social loneliness among females.

A second finding also supports the link between interaction experience and plan effectiveness (Jordan, 1993). In this study, individuals generated plans for the date-request scenario, as well as three other situations. After completing their plans, participants were asked to indicate the extent to which they had taken part in situations like those described in each of the four scenarios. The correlation between the experience ratings and effective-ness judgments of the date-request plans was significant and robust ($r = .70$, $p < .001$). Those reporting higher experience levels in the date-request domain also produced date-request plans that were judged to be more effective. Although another significant correlation ($r = .33$, $p < .03$) was observed between amount of experience and plan effectiveness for one of the other four scenarios, for the remaining two situations, no significant correla-tions were observed between experience levels and plan effectiveness. Be-cause these other three scenarios involved such activities as persuading another person to adopt one's stand on an issue and negotiating with another individual, it is possible that the frequencies with which these types of events occur relative to the frequency with which students request dates is such that there is more variability in the date-request domain, thus promoting a higher correlation between experience and plan effectiveness in this case.

Taken together, these findings suggest explanations that might be pursued in future research to further understanding of the relationships between plan effectiveness and social loneliness. Within the date-request domain, when lonely males are asked to formulate plans for asking females out on dates, they not only find the planning task itself to be cognitively demanding but part of the reason this task is so demanding for them is that they have less prior experience on which to draw to formulate present plans, and, as the latter findings demonstrate, amount of experience is apparently crucial to plan effectiveness in this domain. By contrast, within the roommate ingratiation domain, lonely males tend to be indifferent toward the goal of inducing a new roommate to like them; whereas, within this same domain, lonely females appear to lack the requisite knowledge for accomplishing this goal.

Thus, it appears that the processes underlying the significant correlations between plan effectiveness and loneliness vary both with respect to the goal being pursued and the gender of the individual pursuing the goal. Apparently, lonely males are not particularly motivated to achieve certain social goals (roommate ingratiation), and although they may be motivated to pursue other social goals (date-request), they lack the prior experience necessary to devise effective plans in these domains. Although the date-request goal is of low salience to females in general, their plan effectiveness in this domain increases with experience, probably because they are frequently date-request targets. But their plan effectiveness with respect to requesting dates remains unrelated to their feelings of loneliness because they do not have to act on this knowledge as often as do males to effect this desired social outcome. Within the roommate ingratiation domain, lonely females apparently lack the knowledge necessary to devise effective plans. In general, then, it appears that the mechanisms responsible for producing the relationship between plan effectiveness and loneliness are manifold and involve both cognitive and motivational components.

Cognitive Inefficiency and Plan Effectiveness

As we have seen, for at least some social goals (e.g., requesting a date), the amount of experience one reports having in that domain is directly related to the judged effectiveness of the plans they generate in that domain. As was noted previously, the relationship between the amount of experience one has had in pursuing a specific goal and the level of plan effectiveness in some cases may be masked by the fact that the goal in question is not pursued often enough by most people in the population; so that there is simply not enough variation in experience to correlate with effectiveness. Moreover, it would be shortsighted to assume that experience is the only factor related to plan effectiveness. In fact, it is easy to envision circumstances under which some individuals might accumulate considerable experience in pursuing a specific goal, but their experience might not be particularly informative to them in subsequent attempts to achieve the same goal. This situation could arise if, for example, repeated failures to achieve the goal were surrounded by considerable anxiety and stress—emotional states that could interfere with the analysis and amelioration of potential future failures. People do not always learn from their failures, as the divorce statistics suggest; that is, with each successive divorce, the probability that a subsequent marriage will end in divorce increases rather than decreases.

Clearly, then, although experience can indeed be a teacher, there must be other factors that influence plan effectiveness. One of these potential factors is cognitive inefficiency (Broadbent, Cooper, Fitzgerald, & Parkes, 1982). It is reasonable to suppose that individuals who experience memory failures would not only be less likely to learn from the past failures and thus devise less effective plans; they also should encounter more difficulties in formulating and carrying out present plans. This possibility was tested directly by Jordan (1993); who included a self-report measure of cognitive inefficiency called the Cognitive Failures Questionaire (CFQ) developed by Broadbent et al. (1982) in his planning investigation. These researchers found the CFQ to be positively associated with respondents' spouses reports of the frequency with which respondents demonstrated everyday absent-mindedness. High CFQ scorers also show higher numbers of traffic citations and auto accidents (Larson & Merritt, 1991).

Zero order correlations between the CFQ and effectiveness judgments for plans devised to reach each of four different goals were nonsignificant with one exception ($r = -.33$, p < .03). This situation dealt with persuading another to change his or her mind on an issue. Additional regression analyses revealed that the CFQ did not interact with the amount of experience in pursuing the goal to produce differential plan effectiveness. Although these results suggest that cognitive inefficiency is not a particularly good predictor of plan effectiveness, this investigation did report a significant correlation ($r = .53$, p < .001) between the CFQ and the UCLA Loneliness Scale. Individuals scoring high in loneliness also indicated more of a propensity to experience various kinds of cognitive failures. In view of the fact that plan effectiveness and loneliness tend to be inversely correlated, except when the goal is not one that is frequently pursued (e.g., females in the date-request domain) and the fact that the CFQ is related to feelings of social loneliness but not strongly associated with plan effectiveness, it appears that plan effectiveness and the propensity to experience cognitive failures make independent contributions to feelings of social loneliness. A series of regression analyses confirmed that in no case did plan effectiveness in any of the four domains studied and cognitive inefficiency interact to produce differential levels of social loneliness (Jordan, 1993). Moreover, the evidence offered no support for the possibility that plan effectiveness mediates the relationship between cognitive inefficiency and social loneliness.

In Search of the Holy Grail: Elements of Effective Plans

Although the evidence just reviewed generally supports the notion that the accumulation of experience fosters the development of more effective plans, such a proposal is limited for at least two reasons, one of which has already been spelled out in some detail. First, as noted previously, whereas the data show that the gross amount of experience one has had pursuing the same goal or replanning for the same goal can increase plan efficiency and effectiveness, there are instances in which mere increments in the amount of experience pursuing the goal may not necessarily give rise to improvements in plan effectiveness (e.g., Elizabeth Taylor). Ms. Taylor has been quite effective at finding potential husbands, but she has been terribly ineffective in remaining married to them. Second, from the perspective of providing counsel to those interested in improving the quality of their action plans, the admonition simply to go forth and "experience" seems considerably less than satisfying. As a consequence, the following discussion suggests some potential avenues through which planning effectiveness might be maximized. Some of these possibilities are quite speculative and need to be examined in future research.

Although it may seem somewhat odd, there are those who believe that planning is unnecessary and even may be undesirable when contemplating future goals, as was discussed in chapter 3. Thus, although all normally functioning humans have the capacity for forethought and planning, they may or may not have beliefs that support the potential usefulness of planning activities. Certainly, a prerequisite for effective planning is a belief in the efficacy of planning activity (Kreitler & Kreitler, 1987). Without such beliefs, the activity itself either will not be carried out, or it will be practiced so sporadically that any facilitative, long-term practice effects will be extremely limited. Consequently, the following discussion assumes a system of beliefs that supports planning activities.

Although commitment to planning activities is a necessary condition for developing effective plans, it is clearly not sufficient. Hall (1980) noted that urban and transportation planners, individuals who are planners by profession, frequently devise ineffective and inordinately costly plans. He cited the British–French Concorde supersonic jet transport as one example. In this case, those involved in the project made contractual commitments to build the aircraft before estimates of its full development costs were available. When these estimates were forthcoming, it was too late for these contractual obligations to be broken, and the unanticipated costs had to be born by taxpayers, as they frequently are. The Bay Area Rapid Transit (BART) system in San Francisco is another of Hall's examples. Here again, in order for BART to become a reality, new technology had to be developed, and the project's planners severely underestimated the real costs of the project. In part, these underestimates arose because new and unproved rail technologies were an integral part of BART. It took considerable time and money to debug these technologies once they were in place.

As these and other cases suggest, urban and transportation planners frequently appear to be overly optimistic about the ease with which new technologies can be implemented in their projects. Apparently, there is a very fine line between being "visionary" with respect to a project and devising unrealistic and overly expensive plans to make the project a reality. Of course, in a world in which the profit motive exerts a very strong influence, one can understand how planners might be misled by contractors who claim to be able to produce new technologies at a specific cost, and how planners themselves might be tempted to advance highly ambitious but unrealistic proposals that are attractive to potential clients. Whatever the explanation, the critical point is that even professional planners, whose job it is to devise effective plans, can and do make very large and costly planning blunders.

Prediction is, of course, integral to planning. Because there is considerable evidence to support the claim that individuals routinely are overly optimistic about their abilities to predict future events (Hogarth, 1980), including events that occur randomly, as planners devise and revise plans, they should be alert to this kind of overconfidence in their thinking about the potential success of their plans. It is important to remain highly cognizant of the fact that uncertainty is an integral part of any planning endeavor, and as the planning environment becomes more dynamic and the planning horizon stretches out over time, uncertainty increases. If such parameters produce levels of uncertainty that are excessive, one must question whether it is reasonable to pursue a given goal and thus whether planning is even worth undertaking. In some cases, the best plan may be to wait until the environment in which the goal will be pursued has become more predictable and the goal potentially more achievable within a shorter time span.

Of course, in a given context, urgency may become a significant feature in the planning environment; that is, individuals may believe that a particular goal must be pursued immediately, and a plan must be devised to achieve the goal as soon as possible. However, even in such cases, one must question the immediacy with which the goal in question must be attained. Especially in the domain of social relationships, individuals may have considerably more time than they think to undertake a specific social goal. Again, a default plan that might be useful to invoke in such situations is simply to wait; however, utilizing this default plan presupposes that the time gained will be used to monitor the environment to reduce uncertainty, and to generate a plan once uncertainty has been reduced to the point some degree of prediction is possible. Simply using the time gained by waiting to avoid thinking about the goal in question is not particularly useful, unless uncertainty is so high that it is not worth monitoring the environment at the present time.

When it appears reasonable to launch planning activities, other psychological proclivities must be monitored closely by planners, lest they exert a negative impact on plan effectiveness. Among these is the tendency for individuals to be overly optimistic that a plan they have developed will be successful (Knowlton & Berger, in press; Sherman & Corty, 1984). Knowlton and Berger (in press, Experiments 1 and 2) contrasted the subjective probability estimates of potential success in reaching a goal for those who had devised a plan to achieve the goal with those of individuals who were not given the opportunity to devise such a plan. In both of these experiments, the estimates of success of those who planned were significantly higher than the estimates of those who did not plan. A third experiment in this series produced similar estimated success differences between planning and nonplanning groups that fell short of conventional levels of statistical significance (Knowlton & Berger, in press, Experiment 3).

The effects of the success bias induced by planning activity may be exacerbated when groups of individuals engage in joint planning activities, as Janis and Mann's (1977) research on groupthink indicates. Their analysis of the Bay of Pigs fiasco during the Kennedy administration suggests that the success bias was rampant among those individuals who took part in the discussions surrounding the planning of the invasion. Apparently, there was very little opposition voiced to the invasion goal itself by those involved in the discussion. This potentially disastrous bias can be countered by imagining worst case outcomes, and planning for these contingencies accordingly. Of course, this process of generating worst case scenarios and weighing the relative likelihood of their occurrence may lead to the conclusion that it is not worth pursuing the goal, at least in the near future. Planners must be willing to accept this potential outcome, regardless of their level of commitment to the idea of pursing the goal in question. Furthermore, if such planning is carried out in a group context, it is important to include a number of individuals who are known to be skeptical about or opposed to the notion of pursing the goal or goals in question.

The process of generating worst case conditions that could thwart planned actions presupposes the more general process of mentally simulating plans. Evidence suggests that individuals who produce more efficient plans tend to engage in more of this mental simulation activity than individuals who devise less efficient plans (Battman, 1989; Pea & Hawkins, 1987). Although this evidence seems to support the idea that mental simulation of plans is functional, there is also evidence to suggest that mental simulation of courses of action may increase one's confidence in the likelihood that the course of action will be successful; that is, mental simulation of plans may exacerbate the effects of the success bias. Consequently, as plans are simulated mentally, planners must be aware of the fact that an unanticipated consequence of this process might be overestimation of the potential success of the plan.

In some instances, especially in the social domain, it may be possible to simulate plans in action. Using such techniques as role playing, plans can be realized in a social situation that approximates the one in which the plan eventually will be enacted. Obviously, the usefulness of role playing depends heavily on the degree to which the role play situation is similar to the situation in which the plan ultimately will be carried out. Moreover, here again it is important to involve people in this process who are likely to be unsympathetic to the goal being pursued. Such individuals are likely to respond in ways that force planners to consider both specific contingencies with which they might have to deal when the plan is implemented, and the more general issues of pursuing the goal at all or trying to attain the goal with this particular plan.

Finally, even when plans are being implemented in social action, many times it is possible to make adjustment to contingencies as they arise. Good planners are alert to these opportunities (Hayes-Roth & Hayes-Roth, 1979). Carefully monitoring the environment as the plan is being executed is vital to the success of the plan. In addition to these online adjustments, it is possible to imagine plans that are themselves more amenable to alterations as they are being carried out. The obvious case is plans that contain numerous contingencies, such that when specific actions are blocked, the planner can easily retrieve a readily available action alternative with which to surmount the difficulty. Of course, plans with numerous contingencies are inherently more complex. This characteristic may make the details contained in them more difficult to retrieve as action unfolds in a given social context; however, planners who have the capacity to store and retrieve complex plans containing numerous contingencies must have some advantage in social situations in which actions are likely to be blocked. Of course, the caveat here is that numerous contingencies by themselves do not ensure plan effectiveness. The quality of these alternatives is an issue that also must be considered, and too many alternatives may prove to be debilitating to performance, as the evidence presented in chapter 3 suggests.

Chapter 6

Message Planning Theory and Communication Theory

ᛒ ◆ ᙂ

This chapter addresses two broad issues. The first of these concerns the implications of the plan-based theory explicated in this volume and the research it has spawned for the broader domain of communication theory, especially those theories and models of message production devised by communication researchers. In discussing this issue, I try to show how the theory and research presented in this volume serves to fill some specific lacuna left by these theories and models. The second issue to be addressed concerns the theoretical and empirical gaps that remain unaddressed in the plan-based approach presented here. The primary motivation for undertaking both of these endeavors is to encourage further theoretical integration and empirical inquiry. A detailed discussion of the implications of planning theory for communication practice is reserved for the next and final chapter.

Planning Theory in the Communication Theory Context

A few communication researchers have presented theories or models concerned directly with the cognitive structures and processes subserving action production in general (Greene, 1984b, 1995) and message production in particular (O'Keefe, 1988; O'Keefe & Delia, 1982; O'Keefe & Lambert, 1995; O'Keefe & McCornack, 1987; O'Keefe & Shepard, 1987). In addition to these two bodies of theory and research is the work reported on planning and deceptive communication, some of which was discussed in chapter 3. Other communication researchers have devised models designed to integrate person perception theories with theories of behavior production, with particular reference to nonverbal communication (Patterson, 1983, 1995, in press). Finally, within the domain of mass communication inquiry, functional theories of mass media use (McQuail, 1987), including the uses and gratifications perspective (Katz, Blumler, & Gurevitch, 1974; Palmgreen, Rosengren, & Wenner, 1985), contain postulates and theoretical propositions directly related to goal-directed action and planning. The implications of the plan-based approach for these four areas of communication inquiry are considered in turn.

Action Assembly Theory

Action Assembly Theory (AAT) was first proposed by Greene (1984b) as an overarching theory of action production that might also be invoked to explain some aspects of message production (Greene, 1995). Although the theory cannot be described completely here, there are certain of its features that are germane to planning theory. A central construct of AAT is that of procedural records. These are elemental modular units of procedural memory that specify action and an outcome associated with that action (Greene, 1984b). These modular entities are composed of nodes and associative links. Nodes may provide a symbolic representation of an action, a representation of some outcome associated with that action, or situational features relevant to the action–outcome relationship represented in the record (Greene, 1995). Procedural records are more elemental than complex structures like scripts and plans (Greene, 1984b); however, procedural records may become associatively linked to form complex unitized assemblies that can be retrieved and processed as a single unit. These more complex unitized assemblies are akin to scripts and plans (Greene, 1984b, 1995).

Although it provides an account of the conditions responsible for the activation of procedural records and unitized assemblies, AAT remains mute with respect to the following questions regarding the nature of procedural records and unitized assemblies. First, AAT provides no detailed account of how the degree of articulation or complexity of procedural records or unitized assemblies themselves influence action production. Although Greene (1995) argued that if procedural records and unitized assemblies are not frequently activated or have not been activated recently, they will tend to decay, AAT itself does not address the issue of how such attributes of procedural records and unitized assemblies as their complexity affect the fluidity with which action is produced. The theory does suggest that the instantiation of unitized assemblies and advanced assembly of portions of the output representation will facilitate action production. As the research presented in chapter 3 revealed, the complexity of message plans exerts some influence on the fluency with which these plans are enacted.

Second, AAT does not deal explicitly with the processing complications that may arise from goal failure. This explanatory gap arises from the fact that AAT includes no explicit mechanism that enables individuals to monitor and potentially alter their performance as it unfolds, or to gather information from others regarding their performance for correction purposes; although, in a discussion of cognition and skilled social performance, the importance of such a monitoring function is mentioned (Greene & Geddes, 1993). Although it is not clear why such a monitoring feature was excluded from the theory, clearly, as individuals interact, such monitoring mechanisms come into play, (e.g., when individuals correct their own utterances, or when individuals respond as if they know how their co-interactant had responded internally to what it was they had just said or did). Such message plan monitoring and alteration mechanisms are an integral part of some speech production models (e.g., Levelt, 1989). The theory and research presented in chapter 4 with respect to the hierarchy principle demonstrated the differential cognitive load associated with message plan alterations at different hierarchical levels, and the preference individuals appear to have for low-level message plan alterations.

Finally, AAT does not attempt to address the issue of plan effectiveness. Although retrieval failures, the order in which procedural records or unitized assemblies are activated, and the fluidity with which an output representation is performed may be related to ultimate social effectiveness, these are certainly not the only determinants of competent social interaction performance, as Greene and Geddes (1993) rightly conceded. Thus, one must move beyond descriptions of the structure and processing activities of the cognitive system to consider particular content of the system that may be influential in producing effective messages. For example, as research discussed in chapter 3 indicated, individuals vary with respect to the degree that they have beliefs that support the efficacy of planning, and these beliefs influence the complexity and the potential effectiveness with which they plan (Kreitler & Kreitler, 1987). Moreover, social actors vary with respect to their knowledge about people and social interaction routines. Such individual differences in planning motivation and cognitive content cannot be ignored in a theory of message production that seriously addresses the issue of communication effectiveness.

Furthermore, studies that have allowed individuals to replan action sequences to achieve goals where efficiency can be ascertained in objective terms (e.g., planning a series of classroom chores; Pea & Hawkins, 1987; or a sequences of sales calls; Battman, 1989), have consistently demonstrated that later incarnations of plans are generally more efficient for accomplishing these tasks than are earlier versions. AAT might be invoked to explain why individuals perform more fluently with repeated planning iterations; however, AAT cannot be recruited to account for increments in the quality or efficiency of such plans.

Again, the purpose of this exercise is not to impugn AAT, but to show that there are important facets of the message production process, especially as it unfolds during social interaction, that are ignored by the theory. In general, these gaps arise because the phenomena they entail fall outside of the boundary conditions of the theory (e.g., the theory simply was not designed to explain differential effectiveness). Nonetheless, exposing these explanatory lacuna in AAT suggests the utility of the plan-based approach advocated in this volume.

Message Design Logics

The message design logics (MDL) perspective argues that message producers may pursue multiple goals, single goals, or no particular goals in their interactions with others (O'Keefe, 1988). When multiple goals are pursued in a given interaction, they may vary with respect to their purpose (e.g., an individual seeking a compliance-gaining goal may be simultaneously concerned with the additional goal of not threatening the target of the compliance-gaining attempt). As the number and diversity of goals increase, message producers are faced with an increasingly more complex message-generation task.

The MDL perspective posits a typology consisting of three developmentally differentiated message design logics that individuals may employ to meet these exigencies. These design logics are viewed as implicit theories of communication. The least complex of these implicit theories is the *expressive* design logic. This logic is premised on the idea that "Language is a medium for expressing thoughts and feelings" (O'Keefe, 1988, p. 84). Message producers employing this design logic assume that messages are either true expressions of thoughts and feelings or misrepresentations of them. Potential communication goals beyond expression (e.g., saving face), are not considered by those using this logic, and the criterion for communicative success is clear transmission of thoughts and feelings. This message design logic bears considerable resemblance to Snyder's low self-monitors; whose communication in social situations is predicated on the notion that people should "tell it the way they feel it" (Snyder, 1974, 1987).

A *conventional* message design logic rests on the postulate that communication is a cooperative game played by social rules. In contrast to the expressive logic's focus on self-expression, the key message function pursued in the conventional logic is to produce the desired response cooperatively and within the bounds of social appropriateness. Whereas little attention is paid to message context with the expressive logic, the conventional logic entails the belief that action and meaning are context determined.

Finally, the fundamental premise underlying the *rhetorical* message design logic is that communication is the negotiation and creation of social selves and situations. The primary function of messages under this logic is to negotiate social consensus. Flexibility, symbolic sophistication, and depth of interpretation are valued attributes, and message producers employing this logic "seek to achieve consensus and social legitimation for the reality they speak." (O'Keefe, 1988, p. 88). These three message design logics reflect a developmental progression, with expression posited as the beginning stage. The rhetorical design logic is quite similar to the notion of high self-monitoring, under which social interactors are able to separate thought from action and strategically manipulate their actions to achieve their goals, regardless of their beliefs and feelings (Snyder, 1974, 1987).

A central hypothesis underlying the MDL perspective is that in relatively simple communication situations involving a single goal, the variation in message design logics employed in messages to achieve the goal will be relatively small. In such simple communication situations, the three design logics produce similar messages. However, as the number of goals increases, thus increasing situational complexity (O'Keefe & Delia, 1982), the three logics will produce widely diverse messages (O'Keefe, 1988). One implication of this analysis is that within complex communication situations, where multiple goals are being addressed, the messages produced by communicators employing a rhetorical design logic should be maximally effective in meeting situational demands, relative to communicators using expressive or conventional logics. Furthermore, individuals who employ rhetorical design logic in complex situations should be viewed more positively by others in the situation. O'Keefe and McCornack (1987) tested and found support for this theoretical implication; although, the judgments of messages and message producers reported in this study were not obtained after subjects engaged in face-to-face interactions. Rather, the investigators selected written messages produced by one group of students, who had been asked to respond to a single hypothetical situation, and later gave the messages, so selected, to a second group of students, who read and responded to them in an equally hypothetical context. Other studies that have been influenced by the MDL perspective cannot be described in detail here (O'Keefe & Shepard, 1987; Saeki & O'Keefe, 1994).

Although advocates of the MDL perspective are careful to point out that the three message design logics posited in their typology do not represent enduring, trait-like individual differences that are stable across communication situations (O'Keefe & McCornack, 1987), a significant positive relationship has been reported between interpersonal construct differentiation, presumably a relatively stable individual difference characteristic, and message design logic (O'Keefe, 1988). Individuals who employed a rhetorical design logic in their messages demonstrated significantly higher levels of construct differentiation than did those who manifested expressive and conventional design logics in their messages. Although the construct differentiation mean for conventionals was greater than that for expressives, the difference failed to reach statistically significant levels. This finding suggests the wisdom of a thorough investigation of the degree to which individuals show variation in their propensities to employ one of the three message design logics across a diverse set of communication situations to determine empirically the degree to which these message design proclivities are or are not stable in individuals, as claimed (O'Keefe & McCornack, 1987).

Although O'Keefe (1988) explicitly acknowledged that as goals proliferate in communication situations, the message plans necessary to achieve them must become more complex, the MDL perspective itself is not a planning theory of message production. Rather, this perspective specifies various constraints that may be imposed on the message planning process depending on the particular logic adopted by the message producer. Thus, if a message planner adopts an expressive logic in preference to a rhetorical logic, whether this is a *choice* for message producers with low levels of construct differentiation is unclear, the message designer's planning options are constrained by the characteristics of this implicit theory of communication. However, the MDL perspective neither explicates the message planning process itself nor the nature of the message plans that subserve action; nor does it provide an account of the cognitive structures and processes responsible for the production of messages. What it does suggest is that one planning style (rhetorical) is potentially more effective than the other two (expressive and conventional) in complex communication situations; however, it provides no details about how message plans themselves are structured and how they might be altered if they fail. This latter issue is quite significant, because even when a message producer invokes the rhetorical logic, failure to negotiate a social consensus or a social self may occur. MDL is mute with respect to the strategies of message plan alteration that might follow such goal failures.

The MDL perspective also does not provide a mechanism for explaining how message plans used for recurring situations are stored and retrieved. MDL begins with a goal or set of goals and assumes that the message producer must devise messages anew for each situation. Given the repetitive nature of many everyday communication situations, this is a serious oversight. Arguing that communication situations involving a single goal or no particular goal are inherently less problematic for message producers and thus obviate differences in messages produced by the three design logics does not explain how messages are produced in these less complex and potentially repetitive communication situations. Moreover, less complex communication situations may become problematic for the reasons cited in chapter 4; consequently, it is important to provide a theoretical account for adaptations that may occur in response to goal failures, even in these less complex communication contexts. Although there appear to be some significant gaps in the MDL perspective, unlike AAT, MDL directly addresses issues concerned with communication effectiveness.

In more recent incarnations of the message design perspective, plan-based, problem-solving models of message design (e.g., Appelt, 1982, 1985; Hovy, 1988, 1990) have been rejected in favor of a "local management" approach to message design (O'Keefe, 1997; O'Keefe & Lambert, 1995).

According to these presentations, one significant problem with top-down, problem-solving models is the difficulties they encounter when context-specific exigencies impinge on planners and force them to modulate significantly the abstract act-types as they are instantiated in action. O'Keefe and Lambert (1995) summarized the results of a number of their studies of messages devised to achieve specific instrumental and communication goals that suggest that although recurrent themes may appear in such messages, the messages do not contain evidence of a unitary or coherent strategic structure. Based on these results they aver, "messages are sometimes not functionally unified. A theory that offers only a global characterization of message structure will face difficulty in explaining variability of message forms to message functions" (p. 64).

There are at least two observations that can be made about these claims. First, as noted earlier, planning may proceed in an opportunistic fashion (Hayes-Roth & Hayes-Roth, 1979), such that exigencies unique to a particular context may be taken into account as abstract plans are realized in action. Moreover, some planning theorists (e.g., Alterman, 1988; Hammond, 1989a, 1989b; Schank, 1982) not only explicitly recognize that such context-specific features will demand adjustments when abstract plans are instantiated in action, they also discuss the necessity of altering abstract plans based on the degree to which the plan was or was not successful in achieving the goal or goals in question. Both Schank (1982, 1986) and Hammond (1989a, 1989b) claimed that learning and plan adaptation are failure-driven, and that previous plan failures are used to index plans in memory. Moreover, as discussed at some length in chapter 5, the fact that "replanning" increases the efficiency of plans indicates that even in the absence of implementing a plan in action, mental simulation itself may act to alter plans in significant ways (Battman, 1989; Pea & Hawkins, 1987).

Second, the claim that messages exhibiting a "thematic structure" rather than a "strategic structure" must be the product of a "collation of thoughts" rather than an abstract message plan is at least somewhat suspect (O'Keefe & Lambert, 1995). Simply because the independent clauses contained in messages are coded as "thought units," neither warrants the claims that they are indeed "units of thought" (see Greene, 1990), nor that the absence of a strategic or plan-like structure in a message indicates that an abstract plan was not used to guide the generation of the message. Assuming that the structure of "talk" is isomorphic to, and is an unobstructed conduit to, the structure of thought is more than somewhat tenuous. For example, simply because a message manifests a linear progression of steps to achieve a goal does not rule out the possibility that the message was generated by a hierarchical process (Lichtenstein & Brewer, 1980). Finally, some have suggested a role for plans in connection with speech production processes (i.e., "phonetic plans," Levelt, 1989). Thus, a full understanding of the role message plans play in guiding message production requires the researcher to examine concurrently both verbal and nonverbal message features, not only those manifested in verbal discourse.

It is important to note that this more recent message design account does not deny that message planning takes place. In fact, O'Keefe and Lambert (1995) partially endorsed a speech production model advanced by Hermann (1983) that explicitly depicted interactions between procedural knowledge stored in LTM and the cognitive processes responsible for generating a representation of the current situation. The notions that the generation of messages in context involve the "focusing of thought on knowledge structures" and "collation of thoughts" themselves imply a central role for message plans and message planning in the generation of ongoing social interaction. Abstract message plans indeed may serve as such "collators."

Planning and Deceptive Communication

The general discussion of the relationship between planning activity and action fluidity presented in chapter 3 included a presentation of some studies that have examined the relationship between planning and the degree to which individuals are able to control verbal and nonverbal behaviors during deception (see Miller & Stiff, 1993, for a comprehensive review). The theory and findings included in this presentation suggest at least two significant shortcomings of virtually all of these studies. First, when subjects in these studies were given time to "plan" before engaging in deception, sometimes no manipulation check was included to determine whether they actually planned anything during that time. Second, in most cases subjects were not told exactly what it was they should plan about.

As the theory and research presented in chapter 4 concerning the hierarchy principle suggested, directing attention to message-plan alterations at different hierarchical levels has differential impact on such indicators of cognitive load as speech onset latency. Moreover, as the experimental evidence presented in chapter 4 indicated, the number of alternative plans generated in advance of a failure episode also impacts cognitive load, when individuals are forced to resort to alternative plans. The evidence presented suggested that merely providing individuals with time to "think about a plan" before engaging in interaction without providing them with instructions concerning the specific focus of their planning activity did not produce as dramatic an effect on cognitive load as did the planning manipulations that specifically directed planners to devise multiple plans and required them to do so in the form of maps or written directions (Knowlton & Berger, in press) . Unfortunately, many of the studies of deceptive communication that have included predeception planning manipulations have neither required subjects to produce tangible plans before engaging in deception nor required subjects to focus on planning specific verbal and nonverbal actions.

Moving from such omnibus planning manipulations that simply provide subjects with time to think about a plan to manipulations that demand more focus and the production of a tangible plan might well serve to advance the study of deceptive communication significantly. In preparing to engage in deception in everyday life, individuals can choose to focus their planning efforts primarily on verbal attributes of their deceptive messages or on controlling the nonverbal behaviors that accompany the verbal message. Still other deceptive message producers might try to focus their planning efforts on both of these communication channels simultaneously.

Of course, within these broad verbal and nonverbal communication domains, there are a number of message features that could become the focus of intense planning efforts. In the verbal domain, for example, prospective deceivers might concentrate on specific content details concerning such things as their whereabouts at a particular time, whereas others might focus more on the overall consistency of the story they are about to tell. Here too, some individuals might generate numerous contingencies to anticipate potential deception detection attempts of message recipients. In the nonverbal domain, deceptive message producers might focus their planning efforts on affecting certain kinds of facial expressions and maintaining eye gaze, whereas others might try to control self- and object-focused adaptors by attending to their hands.

Although it is certainly true that directing attentional focus to one verbal or nonverbal message attribute is likely to reduce the message producers' ability to control attributes that are not attended to, the question remains whether focusing on a particular attribute is more likely to make a deceiver more difficult to detect with respect to that attribute. Asking this question, in turn, raises the issue of which attributes of deceptive messages are more crucial to plan for and control with respect to the ultimate effectiveness of the deceptive message. Although some have raised the question of the degree to which familiarity with the target of deceptive messages influences how successful deceivers are (e.g., Miller, deTurck, & Kalbfleisch, 1983), little work has been done to determine how specific knowledge about a target of deception (e.g., how gullible is the target), is integrated into deceptive message plans. Clearly, the availability and types of such knowledge about the target must have some impact on the content and structure of message plans designed to achieve deception goals, especially when the interpersonal stakes are high (diBattista & Abrahams, 1995).

Parallel Process Model of Social Cognition and Social Behavior

Students of social cognition have noted that although social cognitive theories have significant implications for the explanation of social behavior, there have been only modest attempts to link the two (Fiske & Taylor, 1991;

Patterson, in press). In an attempt to redress this situation, Patterson (1995, in press) presented a parallel process model that integrates social perception processes with behavioral production processes, with particular attention to the production of nonverbal behavior. This model posits that biological, cultural, and personality factors primarily affect the choice of social environments within which individuals interact, and determine their habitual patterns of action. Once a specific social interaction environment has been selected and entered, goals, expectancies, affect, dispositions, and cognitive resources influence the initiation of action schemas and the allocation of attention and cognitive effort to various person-perception and behavioral tasks.

The model further argues that as individuals initiate action sequences aimed at achieving situational goals, they simultaneously monitor the appearance and behavior of their co-interactants and use these inputs to make judgments about them. These behavioral and perceptual processes may be run off at varying levels of conscious awareness. Cognitive resources must be used both to accomplish and monitor progress on these behavioral and perceptual tasks, and the distribution of these resources between the two types of tasks may determine the effectiveness of actions taken during the interaction (e.g., excessive monitoring of behavior production might impede perceptual accuracy; Patterson, Churchill, Farag, & Borden, 1991-92).

This parallel process model represents a highly ambitious and heuristically provocative attempt to integrate two heretofore disparate areas of inquiry; however, at this point in time it remains to be tested in its entirety. Furthermore, from the perspective of the theory and research presented in this volume, a potential useful addition to the model would be a feature, similar to the Hierarchy Principle presented in chapter 4, that provides an account of the cognitive and behavioral processes that are activated in the event of goal failure. Clearly, during their interactions with others, individuals are sometimes thwarted in their attempts to reach various instrumental and communication goals. Consequently, models of cognition and social interaction that are purported to be comprehensive must take into account the cognitive and social processes that enable individuals to overcome these barriers.

Plans, Planning, and Media Uses and Gratifications

Functional theories of mass media have had a long history in the study of the processes and effects of mass communication. A detailed review of these specific theories is well beyond the scope of the present chapter (see McQuail, 1987). However, there are a number of basic tenets of the uses and gratifications approach to the study of mass media that are worth considering within the context of the plan-based approach presented here. The five fundamental postulates underlying the uses and gratifications perspective displayed in Table 6.1 were articulated by Katz, Blumler, and Gurevitch (1974).

TABLE 6.1

Five Uses and Gratifications Postulates

1. The audience for mass communication is active and goal-directed rather than passive.

2. Linking need gratification with media choice depends on the initiative of the individual. People use the media rather than being used by the media.

3. The media are but one source of need gratification. Needs may be satisfied by other sources of gratification.

4. Individuals are capable of providing useful self-report data concerning their goals and the ways in which media exposure help satisfy these goals.

5. Value judgments concerning media content and its cultural significance should be held in abeyance while audience orientations are considered.

As these five postulates suggest, the uses and gratifications perspective of mass communication eschews the notion that media affect individuals; rather, the metatheoretical purview subscribed to by the advocates of this perspective argues that individuals use media and other unmediated sources to help them realize their personal goals. Thus, media consumption is an active rather than a passive process; although, one potential goal of media consumption might be simply to "pass time" or "escape" (Greenberg, 1974).

Although it is certainly possible to take issue with one or more of these five postulates (e.g., the degree to which individuals are self-aware enough to provide useful reports concerning their motives and intentions; Berger & Douglas, 1981; Kellermann, 1992; Langer, 1978, 1992; Lewicki, 1986; Uleman & Bargh, 1989), a detailed critique of this perspective and the considerable research literature it has spawned is not presented here (see Palmgreen, Rosengren, & Wenner, 1985). Rather, I show how the plan-based perspective presented in this volume may serve to flesh out the uses and gratifications approach.

Although it is true that the uses and gratifications perspective is concerned with media consumption rather than message production, the idea that message plans themselves may entail the acquisition of information, including media content, for their successful implementation, suggests potential connections between the plan-based theory and the uses and gratifications perspective. Moreover, although the uses and gratifications approach recognizes the goal-directed nature of human action, it provides no account of the processes individuals employ to devise and implement plans to achieve their goals. Thus, although it is instructive to learn that individuals may watch television to compensate for their lack of social interaction (i.e., so-called "parasocial" interaction; Greenberg, 1974), a plan-based approach would require the theorist to assume a broader and inclusive explanatory perspective. Thus, for example, given a group of lonely individuals, the plan-based approach would ask about the plans these individuals might generate to alleviate their feelings of loneliness (see chapter 5). Some of these plans might include watching a favorite TV situation comedy and identifying closely with one or more of its characters as "friends." However, other plans might include no media exposure at all. By definition, these plans would fall outside the purview of the uses and gratifications perspective, but they might very well entail creating opportunities for face-to-face interactions with others.

Although the uses and gratifications approach explicitly recognizes that individual gratifications may be obtained from extra media sources, it has little to say about these sources and how media and nonmedia sources of gratification may interact with each other to produce gratifications. A plan-based view not only demands that such interactions be considered because of its more comprehensive purview, it recognizes that because plans may be differentially effective, individuals may be more or less successful in reaching their goals. Thus, the issues of individual competence and plan effectiveness are explicitly raised by the plan-based approach (see chapter 5).

UNRESOLVED THEORETICAL AND EMPIRICAL ISSUES

Having considered the relationships between the plan-based perspective presented in this volume and extant bodies of communication theory and research, the focus now shifts to potential theoretical and empirical gaps in the plan-based perspective itself. Filling these gaps requires further theoretical elaboration and research.

Acquisition of Plans and Planning Knowledge

The extensive literature on planning cited in this volume has very little to say about how plans and the knowledge that enables people to develop plans are acquired in the first place. Artificial intelligence researchers and cognitive psychologists generally study the influence of plans on memory and action generation by stipulating that individuals have plans available to them in a long-term store, or if not, that they have the capabilities of generating plans. Even developmental psychologists, who have studied children's planning capabilities, generally have not conducted detailed investigations of how children's planning skills develop; although there is some movement in this direction (see Pea & Hawkins, 1987; Siegler & Jenkins, 1989).

Although it is clear that some children are predisposed to believe in the efficacy of planning more than others (Kreitler & Kreitler, 1987), it is not clear exactly why these global differences in planning proclivities arise. Furthermore, although studies that correlate attributes of plans with measures of planning tendencies are useful in revealing broad relationships between individual differences and the products of planning processes, they do not have much to say about the details of planning processes themselves. Only very careful observations of children in the process of planning to reach goals can reveal something about the various planning strategies they use (Pea & Hawkins, 1987; Siegler & Jenkins, 1989); however, even these studies beg the still broader question of how children acquire planning capabilities and beliefs that promote their use. There are many sources of such knowledge including observational learning, generalization from specific episodes in which the child has been an active participant, and direct instruction concerning the importance of planning and how to create plans. Consequently, research needs to be done to determine how children acquire both general planning knowledge and specific plans during their interactions with such socializing agents as parents, teachers, and other children, as well as during their nonsocial interactions with media and the physical environment.

Invisible Plan Hierarchies: The Embeddedness Problem

Throughout this presentation of planning theory and research, a very important issue has been bracketed for the sake of both theoretical parsimony and empirical tractability. This issue has to do with the degree to which local goals and the plans used to pursue them in specific interaction episodes are embedded in still more abstract goal and plan hierarchies that themselves can exert considerable influence on the pursuit of these local goals and plans. This issue was highlighted earlier in the example of consuming food to satisfy immediate hunger, while not necessarily being cognizant of the more abstract goal of sustaining one's life. It is clear that as individuals set about to achieve various concrete goals in their daily lives, they may give little if any thought to the more regnant, abstract goals from which the local subgoals they are pursuing arise.

Within the context of a particular planning study, research participants may be given goals for which to plan that themselves are affected by still more abstract goals. Unfortunately, the influence of these regnant goals is difficult to take into account, even though researchers may be aware of the possible effects they exert on more immediate planning efforts. This is not to impugn studies that, by necessity, have ignored these cascading influences; however, simply because these potential influences can be controlled statistically through random assignment of participants to experimental conditions does not mean that their place in a comprehensive planning theory can be ignored. Many local goals may be pursued in the context of broad, long-term life goals and plans.

Life Plans.

That some individuals engage in large-scale planning projects with lengthy time horizons during certain periods in their lives is a proposition that would seem to be noncontroversial. From relatively young ages, children may begin to speculate about the desirability of pursuing a variety of future occupations, and during high-school years, career concerns may become progressively more prominent. For those who attend college, career decisions may be delayed for some time; however, toward the end of their undergraduate careers, students again are faced with decisions regarding various career paths. Although significant occupational decisions may be made relatively early in life, there are various circumstances that may arise later in life that either allow or force individuals to reconsider earlier choices. Divorce, death, midlife crises, retirement, intense job dissatisfaction, unemployment, empty nests, or any number of other common life events may produce the conditions that necessitate such large-scale planning efforts during later life.

Whether it is a younger individual generating initial career goals, or an older person redefining an extant set of career goals, once such goals are set—either purposively or by default—other subgoals may be engaged automatically. Thus, for example, assuming the requisite level of ability, once a decision is made to become a medical doctor, the educational subgoals implied by this choice are fairly well defined. To attain this goal, a specific educational path is generally followed, beginning with a life science-based undergraduate education, leading to medical school with subsequent clinical experiences, and most likely additional training in a specialty. Whereas some occupational specialties like becoming a lawyer or a dentist also have well-defined subgoal structures in terms of required educational experiences, other occupations, such as working in a retail establishment, imply little in the way of a formal higher-educational subgoal structure for their attainment. For such jobs, some "prior experience" may be the only prerequisite, much to the chagrin of relatively inexperienced youths seeking their first job.

Although this discussion has been dominated by consideration of occupational goals, there are myriad additional, highly abstract, and more ephemeral goals for which individuals can strive (Rokeach, 1968, 1973). Such goals as happiness, personal fulfillment, and eternal salvation may not only become highly conscious on selected occasions for some individuals, they may assume primary and continuing importance. Hedonists, involved in their never-ending search for pleasure, as well as evangelicals, in their pursuit of converts, are among such individuals. Even those with somewhat less extreme proclivities may subordinate occupational goals to such goals as happiness or personal fulfillment such that occupations are chosen or discarded because they are thought to give rise to these desired end states, although some people may see no necessary connection between the two. Moreover, in the domain of social relationships, such goals as developing friendships and romantic relationships clearly may be subordinated to such regnant goals as happiness and personal fulfillment.

It is clear that at certain points in their lives, individuals may step back and ask what it is that would make them happy or happier than they currently feel. By asking these questions, people seek to specify the subgoals that would produce the desired state of happiness, assuming of course that the subgoals can be satisfied. The question is the degree to which planning done in such contexts actually "carries through" to produce the desired end states, or whether such large-scale planning projects are generally so vaguely conceived and involve such lengthy timelines that intervening events subvert their action sequences. This important question deserves research attention.

Life Plan Failure.

Although at certain points in most individuals' lives some attention is likely to be devoted to large-scale planning efforts, much of the time these "megaplans" remain idling in the background, outside of social actors' conscious awareness. It is only when progress toward these more abstract goals is blocked in some significant way that the goals and plans associated with them come into conscious focus. Being unable to complete the education necessary for entering a profession or coming to the realization that during one's lifetime certain desired goals are not likely to be attained are some of the events that could precipitate such conscious awareness.

There are a number of problems that arise when these large-scale plans are called into question. First, as discussed in chapter 2, because these plans may subserve such abstract goals as happiness, their failure should produce significant emotional consequences, many of them negative. For example, the levels of dissatisfaction and unhappiness surrounding so-called midlife crises may be associated with what are judged to be failures of large-scale life plans. That is, individuals may become aware that it is very unlikely that during their lifetimes certain important goals will be attained. By necessity, any strategies for ameliorating these feelings of discontent would have to involve the definition of a new set of goals and the generation of new, large-scale plans to reach them.

A second problem with the failure of these large-scale plans is the sheer magnitude of the task involved in modifying or abandoning old plans and generating new ones. Because these life plans may involve action sequences that are both complex and stretch out over many years, abandoning these sequences and replacing them with alternatives constitutes a relatively daunting planning task for most people. Moreover, as individuals age, they become increasingly aware of the limitations of their future longevity and the inevitable constraints that time limitations place on large-scale redefinition of goals and plans (e.g., deciding to be a physician at 70 years of age after spending a working life as a truck driver). Consequently, one would expect many people experiencing these kinds of failures to feel at least somewhat overwhelmed by the situation in which they find themselves.

A third problem growing out of the failure of life plans is the potential for consequences of these failures to cascade down the plan hierarchy and adversely influence plan-based, goal-directed activity at local levels. Thus, for example, individuals who are unable to complete medical school in their quest to become a physician may find that the disruptive consequences of this failure prevent them from performing everyday, routine goal-directed tasks. Depression and a general lack of self-efficacy (Bandura, 1986) may occur to those who experience large-scale goal failures. These debilitating effects may be relatively short-lived or they may continue to disrupt the individual's life for many years, or until it ends. Exactly why some individuals are able to deal with these negative effects relatively quickly, perhaps by setting realistic goals and generating new plans so that they effectively "move on" in their lives, whereas others remain trapped in prolonged state of paralysis, depression, and personal chaos, is a pressing research issue that needs to be addressed.

Plan Recognition and Counterplanning

As observed in chapter 1, numerous AI models of discourse and text comprehension are predicated on the assumption that individuals gain understandings of the communicative activities of others by making inferences about their goals and the plans they are employing to reach their goals (Black, Kay, & Soloway, 1987; Bower, Black, & Turner, 1979; Carberry, 1990; Cohen, Morgan, & Pollack, 1990; Green, 1989; Levison, 1981; Lichtenstein & Brewer, 1980; Litman & Allen, 1987; Perrault & Allen, 1980; Schank & Abelson, 1977; Schmidt, 1976; Varonis & Gass, 1985; Wilensky, 1983). These inferences about goals and plans make the actions of other individuals understandable, although, of course, these understandings may not be accurate. Although this postulate underlies the design of numerous AI systems intended to comprehend text inputs, and evidence suggests that hierarchically structured, plan-like units appear to organize some types of knowledge in memory (Abbott & Black, 1986; Black & Bower, 1979, 1980; Bower, Black, & Turner, 1979; Cahill & Mitchell, 1987; Lichtenstein & Brewer, 1980; Seifert, Robertson, & Black, 1985), these studies fail to draw explicit links between ongoing actions deployed during social interactions and such inference-making processes. Consequently, a number of fundamental questions, a few of which are illustrated here, remain to be answered.

First, even before individuals encounter each other in a face-to-face interaction, inferential processes may be set in motion in anticipation of the other's likely goals and plans. Thus, the opening interaction sequences of some social encounters may be predicated on goal–plan inferences made well before the interaction commences; for other interactions, such pre-interaction inferencing may not take place. Although it is clear that individuals imagine interactions with others, and these imagined interactions can produce discernible effects (Allen & Edwards, 1991; Allen & Honeycutt, 1996; Edwards, Honeycutt, & Zagacki, 1988, 1989; Honeycutt, 1989, 1991; Honeycutt, Edwards, & Zagacki, 1989-90; Honeycutt, Zagacki, & Edwards, 1992-93), we have relatively little idea of how these anticipatory inferences influence communicative action and how long they survive once the interaction has begun and new information is acquired. How long do such pre-interaction inferences persist as the interaction progresses? How resistant are such inferences to information inconsistent with them? Why do some individuals have the consistent proclivity to attribute malevolent goals to those with whom they interact, whereas others consistently attribute positive motives to others? Clearly, inferences about others' intentions have a profound impact on how one will approach a given encounter with another, and how the interaction is likely to unfold.

Second, once a face-to-face interaction has commenced, a wealth of verbal and nonverbal information is made available to interaction participants. Some AI models of text comprehension postulate that knowledge structures like plans must have some kind of index feature that can be associated with a given environmental cue so that the plan can be activated. For example, Hammond, (1989a, 1989b) argued that frequently used plans are indexed by the goals they subserve. What is not well understood is exactly which verbal and nonverbal interaction features are responsible for activating plans. Most likely it is not any one attribute of verbal or nonverbal behavior (e.g., eye gaze), that activates these knowledge structures, but some configuration of them; that is, certain patterns of verbal and nonverbal action give rise to particular inferences about the goals and plans of the individual producing the action. Little is known about these patterns and the specific processes by which they might activate such knowledge structures as plans.

Third, because humans are capable of making inferences about the future actions of others, they are capable of devising plans to thwart the undesired actions of their fellow interactants (Bruce & Newman, 1978, Carbonell, 1981; Goffman, 1969). Of course, their partners can engage in the same counterplanning activities. The actions and counteractions of Russia and the United States during the cold war are an example of this process on a grand scale. On a much more modest scale, many everyday encounters between individuals may involve similar inferential dances. Employing a strategic, intelligence-gathering metaphor of social interaction, Goffman (1969) asserted that individuals may deploy interaction moves designed to cover their true intentions (*covering moves*), and their interaction partners can enact moves designed to unmask their partners' intentions (*uncovering moves*). However, he also observed that those employing covering moves might anticipate the uncovering moves of their partners and deploy *counter-uncovering moves* to thwart the partners' uncovering moves. Although the logical structure implied in this scheme could be carried out ad infinitum, it is doubtful that in most social, institutional, and governmental interactions, levels of counterplanning and counter-counterplanning beyond those postulated by Goffman occur with great frequency.

These reciprocal inferential processes and the actions predicated on them raise important questions about what is meant by the term *communication*. If people, institutions, or nations mutually adjust their actions on the basis of these reciprocal inference processes, are the inference processes themselves a kind of "interaction?" Mutual adjustments to plans on the basis of no physical interaction certainly constitute a kind of "mutual influence" in the sense that both parties' intentions may be mutually altered on the basis of their inferences about the projected actions of the other (Cappella, 1987). But do such mutual, inference-based adjustments to plans constitute a form of "communication?" Clearly, observation of verbal and nonverbal interchanges between people may or may not be diagnostic of the inferential processes at work as face-to-face interaction unfolds. In this connection, the notion of a so-called "subtext" is akin to the plan construct. Understanding how these two levels of "communication" diverge and converge within the individual and between individuals involved in interpersonal encounters is vital for understanding how social interaction works. Focusing on one of these levels at the expense of the other guarantees limited understanding of interpersonal interaction processes.

Chapter 7

Message Planning
and Communicative Praxis

∞ ◆ ∾

Consistent with the theory and research presented in this volume, Lewin's well-known admonition that good theory is practical, suggestions that the communication field might be profitably viewed as a "practical discipline" (Craig, 1989), the implications of the plan-based theory of message production for the amelioration of some practical communication problems people face in their everyday lives, and some implications of the perspective for the practice of mediated and unmediated communication in everyday situations are considered in turn. Although the theoretical and empirical gaps exposed in the previous chapter may serve to limit our ability to make such extrapolations with complete confidence, there are several significant practical suggestions for improving the effectiveness of communicative action that follow from the theory and research presented in this volume.

MESSAGE PLANNING AND PROBLEM AMELIORATION

When viewed from the perspective of the plan-based approach to message production, a large part of what we generally refer to as individual "socialization" involves, in one way or another, the development and implementation of plans. Beginning at very early ages, children receive instruction from a variety of socializing agents regarding what should be said or done in a wide array of social and nonsocial situations. Children are encouraged to devise plans for many situations they have yet to encounter or may never encounter (e.g., what should be done if a stranger offers a ride while they are walking to or from school, or how they should respond if offered drugs). Because parents and other socializing agents cannot possibly monitor children's behavior during every waking moment, it is critical that children have effective and easily implemented plans readily available for dealing with situations that arise when they must decide and act on their own.

As individuals move from childhood to adulthood, and the amount of guidance they receive from socializing agents decreases, they must rely more and more on their own plans and planning abilities for dealing with everyday situations. This movement toward greater independence and self-reliance presupposes that the individual has developed effective plans to cope with many contingencies that may have to be faced during adult life, including aging and death. Unfortunately, these prerequisites are not always met. For example, some couples experiencing unwanted pregnancies because of profound lack of basic knowledge about human reproduction and birth control (e.g., holding the belief that conception is not possible during a full moon), can hardly be expected to devise very effective plans for preventing pregnancy. In this particular example, it is worth noting that knowledge of human reproduction is a necessary but not a sufficient condition for claiming that one has a "plan" to prevent pregnancy; such a plan would obviously have to embody considerably more than mere knowledge of how reproduction works. People may have perfectly effective plans for dealing with a given contingency and, for a variety of reasons, fail to implement them (e.g., "We just got carried away").

At this point in time there are only a few specific examples of the application of the plan-based theory to practical communication problems, but the reader no doubt will be able to generate many more. Two such applications are considered here, with the hope that these cases will encourage others to consider this approach for dealing with other problems that confront individuals in their everyday social commerce.

AIDS Prevention and Safer Sex

Health communication researchers have devoted increasing energy to studying various communication issues surrounding the HIV/AIDS outbreak (Edgar, Fitzpatrick, & Freimuth, 1992). In particular, although considerable attention has been focused on the role communication plays in encouraging individuals to engage in "safe sex" or, more appropriately, "safer sex," some have noted that little is known about the plans individuals may or may not have regarding condom use during sexual intercourse to prevent the transmission of HIV (Metts & Fitzpatrick, 1992). It is obvious that within the context of highly emotionally charged sexual encounters, a very complex set of factors, including those associated with plans and planning, determine whether or not condoms will be used.

Although not addressing the issue of condom use directly, one study has examined the relationship between message-plan abstractness and the ability of individuals to elicit AIDS-related information from others (Waldron, Caughlin, & Jackson, 1995). In this study, pairs of individuals discussed the AIDS issue, and one of the participants in each dyad was given the objective of eliciting as much information about AIDS from his or her partner as possible. At the conclusion of the conversation, discussants completed a cued-recall procedure, in which they individually reviewed a videotape of their interaction (Cegala & Waldron, 1992; Ickes, Robertson, Took, & Teng, 1986; Waldron, 1990; Waldron, Cegala, Sharkey, & Teboul, 1990). When they could recall what they were thinking or feeling at a given point in the conversation, they stopped the videotape and noted the thought or feeling.

The thought lists generated by the research participants were coded for evidence of plans at four different levels of abstraction, ranging from implementation-level plans (highly concrete) to undifferentiated plans (highly abstract), including a category reflecting no evidence of plans. The videotapes were also scored for the specificity of AIDS-related information obtained by the information seekers. Analyses of these measures revealed that those information seekers who demonstrated evidence of more concrete plans in the cued-recall procedure elicited significantly more specific AIDS-related information from their partners than those whose plans were less specific and those who showed no evidence of planning during the interaction. Analyses also showed that those whose plans contained more actions elicited more specific AIDS-related information from their partners.

Although this study did not focus specifically on plans for condom use during sexual encounters, it suggests that the degree to which plans embody representations of concrete actions may be related to the effectiveness with which they are implemented during conversations. Apparently, within this experimental context, implementation-level plans were more effective in eliciting information than their more abstract counterparts. This finding suggests that the effectiveness of plans for condom use that might be employed during sexual encounters may also depend on the degree to which they include specific and concrete actions. However, this hypothesis requires further evaluation in a study that focuses specifically on condom use.

Alleviating Loneliness

The discussion of plan effectiveness presented in chapter 5 included two studies that demonstrated significant relationships between plan effectiveness, as determined by judges ratings, and loneliness (Berger & Bell, 1988; Berger & diBattista, 1992a). These studies provided evidence that these relationships tend to hold when differentially effective plans are actually implemented. Thus, finding significant correlations between the effectiveness of date-request plans and loneliness among only males suggests that, even though the effectiveness of females' date-request plans may vary, the fact that they do not usually request dates nullifies any plan effectiveness–loneliness relationship among them within this domain of social activity.

As pointed out previously, based on the correlational evidence presented in these two studies, it is difficult to argue that ineffective plans for accomplishing such social goals as date-requesting are causes of loneliness; it is equally plausible to assert that loneliness may be caused by other factors, and may itself be a cause of ineffective plans. In all probability, ineffective plans and loneliness feed reciprocally on each other, each assuming a causal role at different times. Nonetheless, it is worth entertaining the possibility that one way to ameliorate loneliness might be to teach lonely people more effective plans for interacting with others, assuming, of course that the lonely individuals wish to interact with others. Such plans might include entering into activities that are likely to increase the number and range of social contacts (a tennis group vs. a solitary activity), initial interaction plans for meeting strangers, and action sequences for developing friendships and romantic relationships.

It is now well-established that there are socially shared communication plans that embody routines for becoming acquainted with strangers (Berger & Kellermann, 1983, 1989; Kellermann, 1991, 1995; Kellermann & Berger, 1984; Kellermann, Broetzmann, Lim, & Kitao, 1989; Kellermann & Lim, 1990). This is not to say that such plans are themselves sufficient for success, even if they are potentially effective; well-conceived plans may fail because of implementation problems. Nevertheless, effective plans are vitally necessary for interpersonal effectiveness. As the discussion presented in chapter 5 indicated, at this juncture we are not in a position to stipulate, a priori, what effective plans might be; however, our research indicates that judges reliably perceive such effectiveness differences in plans and these judged differences have important and meaningful social consequences.

Although not conducted within the domain of initial interactions between strangers, the developmental research reported by Kreitler and Kreitler (1987) indicated significant increases in plan complexity with increasing age. This finding suggests the possibility of establishing at least rough age norms for plan complexity. Assuming that initial interaction plans show the same age-related increases as the kinds of plans studied by Kreitler and Kreitler (1987), it might be possible to identify individuals whose initial interaction plans are not as elaborate as would be expected for an individual of that age. If the question of how effective and ineffective plans tend to differ can be answered successfully, perhaps effective initial interaction plans can be "taught." Of course, the same could be true for plans devised to reach a number of other social goals.

There is at least one caution that needs to be introduced here regarding age-related changes in plan complexity, however. Recall that Jordan (1993) found a significant and moderately strong positive correlation ($r = .70$) between the reported amount of experience in requesting dates and the rated effectiveness of date-request plans; that is, individuals with more date-request experience developed plans that were judged by others to be more effective. Moreover, in a study that reported similar findings, Berger and Bell (1988) found significant positive correlations between class rank and the rated effectiveness of date-request plans for both males and females (r_{males} = .41; $r_{females}$ = .39). Given that date-request experiences should accrete over a four-year college career, then in this study class rank was probably a reasonable surrogate for amount of date-request experience. Taken together, these findings suggest that it is the amount of experience one has in the date-request domain that may be more critical to the development of effective date-request plans than age. Clearly, individuals of the same age have highly variable amounts of date-request experience; thus, age per se may not be the crucial variable to monitor in terms of developmental progressions in plan complexity.

MESSAGE PLANNING AND COMMUNICATION PRACTICE

The preceding discussion focused on two specific goals that more effective plans might help to achieve. There are, of course, a host of additional possibilities that cannot be considered here. The remainder of this chapter is devoted to a more general discussion of the role plans and planning play in the practice of communication, including common contingencies that must be taken into account when planning for and participating in everyday communication episodes.

Goal Attainability

Because the theory and research presented in this volume have taken it as a given that individuals have goals they wish to pursue, even when they are thwarted in doing so, it is important to recognize that in many situations individuals must decide whether pursuing a particular goal or set of goals is a reasonable course of action in the first place. No attempt is made here to explicate a theoretical account of how individuals go about assessing the attainability of goals, but surely such assessments must be made. Of course, experience teaches us that these individual determinations may be significantly flawed and highly unrealistic, as in the case of the tone-deaf individual who spends considerable time, money, and effort seriously pursuing a professional career as an opera singer, or the person who has extremely limited mathematical skills who attempts to initiate a career as a professional engineer.

Because planning can be demanding of both time and energy, and even though canned plans may be retrieved and utilized virtually automatically, it is reasonable to suppose that before scarce resources are expended on planning and plan implementation, some assessment of the degree to which a goal or goals can be achieved is made. If individuals calculate that a goal or set of goals is unattainable, they must determine further whether this is a permanent or temporary condition. A rudimentary plan for dealing with social situations in which a goal or goals seem unattainable at the present time is simply to wait until the conditions seem to be more favorable for pursuing the goal or goals (e.g., waiting until a target individual is in a better mood before requesting a favor). However, there may be circumstances under which a goal or goals must be abandoned forever (e.g., realizing that at the age of 50 it is very unlikely that one will be able to embark successfully on a career as a professional football player in the National Football League). It is crucial for planners to recognize these practical limitations, lest they squander scarce planning resources on goals that have a very low or no probability of being realized.

Inevitable Uncertainties

Efforts to devise message plans, either before a communicative episode commences or online as interaction unfolds, must take place in a context where there is explicit and continuing recognition that both people and situations change, sometimes radically, rapidly, and unpredictably (Berger, 1995b, 1997). The initial goals, plans, beliefs, and affective states of individuals with whom one interacts while attempting to achieve focal goals may be discrepant with planners' expectations. Even if these initial expectations are met at the beginning of the communication episode, these goals, plans, and affective states may be altered during the course of the encounter. Generating message plans in an atmosphere of certitude about others' goals, plans, beliefs, and affective states is likely to render the plans, so devised, less than effective and potentially counterproductive. Or, as Francis Bacon (1605/1975) wisely observed, "If a man will begin with certainties, he will end with doubts; but if he will be content to begin with doubts, he shall end in certainties" (p. 80). As noted previously, the propensity for individuals to become more confident of their ability to attain focal goals after they have developed a plan, which itself may or may not be effective (Knowlton, 1994; Knowlton & Berger, in press; Sherman & Corty, 1984), may fuel overconfidence about the potential success of the plan and lead to underestimation of the degree to which attributes of the situation within which the plan will be enacted, and attributes of the individuals who will be encountered therein are variable and potentially unpredictable. In many planning contexts, underestimation of such variability may be an important factor contributing to plan failure.

In addition to being aware of the tendency for those who have devised a plan to be more confident that they will achieve their goal, so that these expectations can be adjusted downward to arrive at potentially more reasonable estimates of plan success, individuals can meet the uncertainties associated with planning using additional methods. First, as observed in chapter 2, these uncertainties may be taken into account by devising only abstract, partial plans, the details of which are filled in as action unfolds (Bratman, 1987, 1990). A potential by-product of this partial planning strategy might be to ameliorate the success bias, because planners using this approach must explicitly recognize that there are potential uncertainties lurking in the future. Of course, research contrasting the confidence levels of those employing different planning approaches would itself be necessary to answer this particular research question with greater certainty.

Second, it was observed in chapter 2 that planners can build contingencies into their plans as a way of coping with uncertainty; however, the research evidence adduced in chapter 3 suggested that when such highly complex plans are thwarted, action fluidity may be adversely affected. It may be that contingent planning is most efficient when uncertainty is moderate. When uncertainty is low, contingent planning would not seem to be very fruitful, because planners can be more certain that specific actions are likely to produce specific effects. Under conditions of very high uncertainty, attempting to delineate explicitly all contingencies would seem to be a futile exercise. In the case of high uncertainty, partial plans that are "filled in" as the situation unfolds would seem to have greater utility. However, in cases where there is a relatively small number of potential alternative contingencies that could occur, it might be productive both to plan in greater detail and to explicitly map contingent actions in the event of plan failure, while recognizing that it is probably impossible to delineate all potential contingencies in advance.

Third, whether planners enter communication episodes armed with detailed or sketchy plans, because these episodes are, by their nature, quite dynamic, they must be adaptive to changing circumstances. Being adaptive in this context means that interacting planners must recognize changes in relevant goals, plans, beliefs, and affective states of their partners, and alter their plans on the basis of these perceived changes. These adaptation processes may involve "second-guessing" (Hewes, 1995; Hewes & Graham, 1989). In fact, it is reasonable to postulate that these adaptive processes themselves can be plan-guided. Knowing what to "look for" to detect changes in goals, plans, beliefs, and affective states; how to determine whether these changes are "real" and potentially consequential for goal achievement; and what aspects of plans to alter in response to these changes in order to facilitate the attainment of focal goals, all could be part of "adaptation plans" that contain requisite knowledge for achieving these goals. Clearly, in most cases it is not enough to have an action plan, no matter how well thought out, to achieve a goal. In many cases, plans that guide these adaptation processes are necessary for these action plans to be implemented successfully (Alterman, 1988).

Finally, high uncertainty levels in social encounters can be dealt with by employing message plans that place the interaction onus on those with whom one is interacting. For example, encouraging conversational partners to talk about themselves serves at least two potentially useful functions in this regard. First, by encouraging disclosive behavior from partners, planners may acquire useful information for further specifying their own message plans; that is, information disclosed by partners may help to "fill in" partial plans (Berger & Kellermann, 1994). Second, by placing the conversational focus on the partner, planners can "buy time" in which to develop their own message plans in greater detail. Under most conditions, it is probably considerably more difficult to engage in conscious planning activities when one assumes the speaker role during a conversation. Of course, there is the possibility that interactants who devote conscious attention to planning their subsequent messages while in the listener role risk the potential embarrassment of being "caught not listening" to what has been just said by their partners. Nonetheless, there seems to be little doubt that the listener role affords the individual greater opportunity for further message planning.

No matter how carefully message targets are assayed by message producers, and no matter how carefully messages are planned and crafted before they are disseminated to targets, there is virtually always some measure of residual uncertainty concerning the potential effects of the message on the target. Given this residual uncertainty, it is reasonable to suppose that message producers have at their disposal various hedges that they may use to protect themselves from unanticipated negative consequences that may accrue from deploying a particular message.

Berger (1988a) found evidence for one such hedge in the context of date-request scenarios. In this study, the date-request plans of a few males included an element indicating that the entire date-request episode should be carried out within a humorous frame. The logic underlying this frame was that if the individual being asked for the date refused the request, thus raising the ugly specters of face loss and embarrassment for the requester, the requester could save face by indicating that he was "only kidding" and he really was not serious about asking for the date. Devices like these can be included in message plans to protect the message producer against the down-side risks of unpredicted negative outcomes.

Critiquing Plans and Goals

Another avenue by which the success bias associated with the development of plans can be reduced is by explicitly raising questions about the effects specific actions contained in formulated plans are likely to produce, if the plans are implemented (Berger, 1988c; Berger, Karol, & Jordan, 1989). This critical process may expose unanticipated consequences that may arise when the plan is implemented, or significant gaps in the plan that remain to be filled in before the plan is used. Moreover, depending on the nature of the consequences and gaps discovered by employing this critical process, estimates of the degree to which goals may be attained by implementing the plan may be revised significantly and in a more realistic direction.

For this critical process to be effective, however, planners must be able to assume a skeptical attitude about plans that they may have expended considerable time and energy developing. Given significant investments of time and energy, planners may become so emotionally tied to their plans that they are unable to assume a critical attitude toward them. As was pointed out earlier, these tendencies to be uncritical may be exacerbated in the context of collaborative planning. In such situations, individuals are frequently explicitly admonished by colleagues to "get with the program" and be "team players" in order to work toward a common goal or goals. However, whereas the "team player" concept may be highly functional at the point of plan implementation, the kind of "group think" mentality implied by this notion, with its attendant noncritical cast, may influence planning processes in ways that produce neither close to optimal nor effective plans (Janis & Mann, 1977).

When individuals generate plans involving highly affect-laden goals that have potentially significant consequences in terms of one's life (e.g., getting married or divorced), it is especially important for these planners to step outside of themselves and invite criticism of their plans from external agents. The affective "pull" of such goals may be so great that it impairs planners, so "pulled," to assume a critical attitude toward the plans they have devised for reaching these goals. However, finding critics who are willing to raise potentially difficult questions about the plausibility and desirability of various planned courses of action may prove to be difficult. For example, the strategy of employing close friends as critics may not be as useful as it may seem. Although close friends may know the planner well and be both available and willing to play the critic role, they may be reticent to offer candid reactions to plans and goals because they fear their friendship with the planner will be jeopardized if their assessments are highly critical. Of course, there are those who would contend that a "true friend" is one who would offer candid assessments to the planner, no matter how difficult and challenging the reactions might be. Although this certainly rings true as a potential ideal, in practical terms, concerns for preserving a friendship or other close relationship may undermine the degree to which critiques of friends' plans are both cogent and incisive.

To make matters still more complex, some "implicit theories" of relationships and friendships may define the role of friend-as-critic quite differently. For example, what might be dubbed "The Unconditional-Love School of Relationships" subscribes to a credo advocating a noncritical stance toward the goals, plans, and actions of friends and loved ones. Within this purview, friends and loved ones should be in the business of "supporting" each other's individual projects, whatever they may be, at least up to a point. In the present context, a friendship or relationship erected on this kind of scaffolding would seem to offer little in the way of critical help to the individual planner. By contrast, individuals matriculated in the "Open-and-Honest School of Relationships" might provide considerably more pointed criticism.

In the process of critiquing plans, questions may arise about the attainability of goals, a topic considered earlier. Furthermore, another equally important issue that may surface as the result of plan critique concerns the desirability of pursuing the goal or goals that the plan is designed to achieve. Here the question is not one of the plausibility of the plan for attaining the goal, but one of the degree to which the goal itself is worth pursuing. In the context of a decision to marry, for instance, a critic might agree that the friend's plan will probably bring about the intended result, (i.e., being in a state of matrimony with someone), but the critic may raise the additional question of why the friend wants to get married in the first place. In this case, the critic might encourage the planner to consider how the marriage goal fits into a broader life plan designed to achieve an even more regnant goal (e.g., self-fulfillment or happiness). The critic might point out that even a happy marriage may not be self-fulfilling, or that a happy marriage that is relatively conflict-free may not contribute very much toward the overall happiness goal. If the planner's retort to these suggestions is that being single produces more feelings of "loneliness" than having a close, long-term relationship with someone, the critic might reply that a state of "nonloneliness" may be achievable outside of marriage. Again, the issue here is not one of the plausibility of the plan itself, but the extent to which the goal is desirable and will act to promote or hinder the achievement of other, more abstract goals. Thus, this procedure is a potential antidote to the embeddedness problem explicated in the previous chapter.

Critics must be careful when raising questions about goals and plans, because such questions are in some ways akin to the goal blocks discussed in chapter 2. Recall that these goal blocks are likely to give rise to negative affect, depending on such factors as the amount of time and effort the individual has already expended toward reaching the goal, and how close he or she is to reaching the goal, at least in a psychological sense. In the present case, the magnitude of negative affect manifested in response to plan or goal critique may increase according to the amount of time and effort already invested in developing the plan to reach the goal, rather than the number of overt actions taken to attain the goal. Moreover, based on the previous analysis, we would expect that as the importance of the goal and the estimated probability of success of the plan increase, the amount of negative affect generated in response to critiques of plans and goals also will tend to increase. Consequently, an individual asked to play the role of goal/plan critic would be well advised to approach this task with considerable trepidation, especially when the planner requesting the critique has spent considerable time devising the plan for an important goal, the planner is highly confident of the plan's likely success, and the planner has already invested time and effort in the plan's implementation.

It is difficult to provide critics with specific suggestions for avoiding the induction of negative affect in planners who request their help under these circumstances. However, a general plan for dealing with such difficult situations is to avoid being evaluative (e.g., "This sounds like a bad idea to me"), and simply raise questions of the order, "Have you thought about the possibility of...?" with respect to planned actions, goals, and potential unanticipated consequences. Of course, if the critic raises these questions at every turn, the planner is likely to conclude that the critic is negatively predisposed toward the plan, the goals being pursued, or both. Consequently, the critic must limit the number of these challenges.

Moreover, given that planners tend to be preoccupied with working out the details of the plans themselves, and as a result may be blind to more abstract goals and plans, critics may be able to help planners regain some perspective by helping them view their specific goals and plans within the context of broader goals and plans. This can be accomplished by asking questions that direct planners to think in these broader terms (e.g., "How will achieving this goal help you attain the goal of _____?" or more indirectly, "Why do you want to achieve this goal?").

Another potential consequence of goal-plan critiques concerns the moral and ethical dimensions of goals and the actions taken to achieve them. In the course of describing goals and proposed plans to achieve them, critics may raise questions about the "rightness" or "wrongness" of both goals and the actions contained in plans. It is possible, of course, that planners may become aware of such moral and ethical issues as they individually devise their plans; however, an outside critic might see more clearly aspects of goals and plans that are morally or ethically questionable and feed these judgments back to planners.

Here again, some critics may find it difficult to participate in this process because of the negative affect their feedback may potentiate in planners. If the critic provides such feedback to planners, no matter how such judgments are couched, the implicit message to planners is that they have considered engaging in what the critic judges to be potentially immoral or unethical conduct. Of course, the saving grace for the planner is that considering such conduct is not the same as carrying it out. Regardless of the affective consequences for the planner, there are clearly instances in which planners and critics may have to act to reject goals and plans that fall outside the bounds of acceptable moral and ethical standards of conduct.

Plan Traps

The notion that through frequent and successful application, plans may become represented in long-term memory as canned plans, has been noted at several points in this presentation (Hammond, 1989a, 1989b). Obviously, great cognitive efficiencies are gained by representing frequently used action sequences in memory this way. Undertaking conscious planning to achieve a multitude of everyday goals as they arise would virtually freeze social actors in an almost never-ending state of planning. However, the canning of plans and the actions they automatically guide on cue come at some costs. The practical planner should be appraised of these risks.

First, those concerning themselves with the study of action slips have adduced considerable evidence to suggest that under some conditions, extant knowledge structures may be activated in such a way that they are inappropriate for achieving the local goals pursued by individuals (e.g., people who find themselves in a room but fail to remember why they have come there, or individuals who intend to change their clothes before having dinner but instead put on their pajamas by mistake; Norman, 1981; Reason, 1990). Although the origins of these and other action slips cannot be sorted out in detail here, it is important to remember that highly practiced, canned plans may be subject to faulty activation and because they are well practiced, they may be run off to ridiculous lengths with potentially disastrous results before the problem is detected.

Second, a somewhat less extreme possibility concerns situations in which canned plans are applied appropriately, but lose their efficiency, effectiveness, or both over time because of subtle and slow changes in the environment in which the plan is typically implemented. Social actors employing canned plans may be insensitive to these subtle changes because their canned plans have worked so well in the past. In this sense, planners may become trapped by prior successes, as did the captains of the American automobile industry who, at the time of the 1973 Arab oil embargo of the United States, assumed that Americans would not be willing to purchase small, fuel-efficient automobiles made in Japan. In this case, the fact that American consumers had purchased large, fuel-inefficient automobiles in the past was taken as evidence that they would continue to do so. It was not until Japanese imports began to capture an increasing share of the new car market in the United States that automobile industry leaders realized their miscalculation and became serious about producing high-quality, fuel-efficient automobiles.

On a much smaller but no less important scale, this same phenomenon may afflict individuals involved in long-term relationships. Assuming that what has pleased their relationship partner in the past will continue to do so in the future would seem to promote insensitivity to change and, as a result, potentially negative consequences for the stability of the relationship. Thus, giving similar gifts every year on a particular occasion may provoke both difficult-to-understand disappointment and accusations of insensitivity to change when the gift recipient's preferences show subtle shifts over time. Expressions of disappointment by the recipient in this context are especially frustrating because the objective of giving the gift is to bring pleasure to the receiver. Being entrapped by old plans in dynamic environments may potentiate such undesirable consequences, even when the changes in the environment are relatively gradual.

The possibility that disjunctions between old plans and the requirements of the present environment can develop over time suggests the wisdom of re-examining old plans to determine whether they are as effective or efficient as they once were, even as they continue to produce desired outcomes. When plans successfully bring about desired end states, the positive affect resulting from goal achievement may direct attention away from monitoring the plan itself and to "basking in the glory" of goal attainment. The experience of this positive affect after success is both understandable and in some ways desirable, as such positive feelings may help to bolster self-esteem and self-confidence in the long term. However, remaining in this highly positive emotional state for a prolonged period of time may act to sow the seeds of future plan failures, especially if the euphoria associated with success interferes significantly with the detection of change in the environment and the monitoring of the plan itself. Only when the euphoria subsides may the planner discover that plans have been rendered obsolete by environmental change, and this discovery may come too late.

Action Fluidity and Social Judgment

Although planning theory is centrally concerned with the production of action, including action that is communicative, plans and planning have action consequences that may influence other social agents' perceptions and judgments of planners. In chapters 2 and 3 the relationships between plan complexity and action fluidity were considered in some detail, and it was noted briefly that the fluidity with which action is produced may affect others' judgments of actors. Co-interactants' responses to the fluidity with which these actions are performed may feed back to message producers and influence their subsequent message plans and the actions flowing from them.

There is considerable literature that has examined the links between nonverbal behaviors and perceivers' judgments of those emitting these behaviors. In an early study of these relationships, Miller and Hewgill (1964) reported that individuals who demonstrated more verbal nonfluencies in their speech were judged by others to have lower levels of competence and dynamism than their more verbally fluent counterparts; however, variations in verbal fluency were unrelated to perceivers' judgments of trustworthiness. Wiemann (1977) reported that individuals who included more nonvocalized pauses in their speech and interrupted their partners more, as well as changed conversational topics unilaterally were judged to be less communicatively competent than those who showed fewer of these features in their speech and interaction behavior. However, because these disruptions were manipulated in concert, it is difficult to know the precise role that speech disruptions themselves played in undermining competence judgments.

A number of additional studies have found similar relationships between various speech disruptions (e.g., vocalized pauses, nonvocalized pauses, and false starts), and perceivers' judgments of communication competence, attractiveness, and source credibility. For example, stepwise regression analyses reported by Burgoon, Birk, and Pfau (1990) found that a verbal fluency measure consisting of repetitions, nonfluencies, sentence changes, sentence incompletions, and stuttering was the only significant predictor of competence ratings of individuals presenting persuasive speeches. Other kinesic and vocalic cues given by the speakers failed to predict competence judgments. The competence judgments also were found to be significant predictors of the source's persuasiveness. The verbal fluency index was also a significant predictor of the source's overall sociability and persuasiveness.

Although it is tempting to conclude from this very brief overview that decreased action fluency, especially that associated with verbal fluency, is likely to undermine social judgments of various kinds, thus reducing the potential communication effectiveness of the dysfluent individual, there is at least one important limitation to much of the research reported concerning these relationships. In most of these studies, judges were presented stimulus materials depicting the verbal and nonverbal behavior of total strangers; that is, the individuals emitting the behaviors that judges observed were completely unknown to the judges. Although these procedures have much to recommend them in terms of experimental control, their use limits the generalizability of these findings to those interactions involving total strangers. These limitations are not inconsequential.

It may be that under some conditions, reduced action fluency may not undermine social judgments, especially when those making the judgments have prior information about the stimulus person. For example, individuals' judgments of the competence of a Nobel prize winner may be little influenced by high levels of vocalized pauses emitted during a lecture by the Nobel laureate. In fact, marked lack of action fluency may be taken as a sign of extreme thoughtfulness and intelligence. Moreover, because in this kind of situation the audience is likely to be focused on the content of the presentation, the influence of these disruptions and other similar peripheral cues may be minimized (Petty & Cacioppo, 1981, 1986). Of course, at the other extreme is the possibility that those who are highly fluent may be judged by some to be too "slick."

In spite of these potential exceptions, because there are clear-cut relationships between plan complexity and the levels at which message plans are altered on the one hand, and action fluency on the other, and because there are clearly discernible relationships between action fluency and social judgments, message planners should be concerned with the degree to which the fluidity of their actions will be affected by the message plans they develop and the potential contingencies they may encounter while deploying them. Given the theory and research discussed in chapters 2 and 3 with respect to these relationships, either very simple or overly complex message plans that fail are likely to be associated with decreased action fluidity. Decrements in action fluidity, in turn, may adversely influence various judgments of the message producer by those who witness these action dysfluencies. Consequently, from this perspective, being overly prepared for goal-directed communication encounters may be as potentially dysfunctional as being under-prepared for such communication situations.

Planning Versus Spontaneity

It may appear to be somewhat paradoxical that, on the one hand, humans are endowed with the capability of forethought and planning, but, on the other hand, are prone to cognitive sloth (Fiske & Taylor, 1984, 1991). Given the human capacity for planning, why are some individuals not only loath to use this capacity but suggest that planning is undesirable because it undermines individual creativity, spontaneity, and expressiveness? The stereotype of the planner created by such planning critics is one of a highly risk-averse "nerd," who devotes considerable time to calculating in advance even the most inconsequential actions, and rigidly follows the resulting plan with little or no deviation. As a consequence, these mechanical "plodders" are dull and boring people to encounter socially precisely because they lack the spontaneity that makes people both "unique" and "interesting." In a culture that emphasizes individuality and the attendant attributes associated with this orientation, planning as an activity may be a particular anathema. Because planning requires both time and mental effort and because planning may be perceived to produce socially dull and uninteresting individuals, there are very strong social pressures that may countervail against planning as an activity.

Begging the question of whether these antiplanning caricatures of planners contain any truth at all, looking at this issue from a broader perspective provides an alternative to this simplistic and bifurcated way of thinking about planning and spontaneity. Specifically, it is reasonable to suggest that under some circumstances, planning itself enables spontaneity. This is true in at least two senses. First, planning may make goal-directed action more efficient, thus enabling social actors to use these time savings to engage in more spontaneous pursuits. Those who fail to plan may spend more time achieving the same goals and have less time to engage in more spontaneous action. Thus, for example, those who have planned well for their retirement years are more likely to have significantly more free time to do what they please than those who have not so planned and, as a result, may be faced with the unpleasant prospect of working until they no longer are able.

Second, spontaneity itself may be planned. As has been emphasized throughout this volume, actions may be plan-guided without being consciously planned in advance. The fact that some actions are recognized by social observers to be "spontaneous" suggests that we have "plans" that enable us to recognize actions that appear to be unplanned. Furthermore, it is difficult to conceive of purposive action arising from a *tabula rasa*. Certainly, some cognitive structures and processes are implicated even in the production of what appear to be highly "spontaneous" actions. Consequently, what pass for spontaneous actions themselves may be plan-guided. Thus, as individuals act in accordance with their plans, and they encounter plan thwarting actions from their co-interactants, they may enact alternative *planned actions* that appear to observers to be "spontaneous."

If this line of argument has some measure of merit, it seems possible that individuals could be taught plans that would enable them to be more "spontaneous." For example, such plans might stipulate that when meeting someone for the first time, there is a range of appropriate conversational topics that can be broached and some topics that are taboo. The "spontaneous" part of the plan would entail choosing from the alternatives bounded by this range in any specific conversation. Given this view, it is possible to be spontaneously appropriate or spontaneously inappropriate during such a conversation, a contingency that itself should give antiplanning advocates considerable pause. Clearly, spontaneity, whatever it is, is not an unmixed communicative blessing. In any event, part of what it means to be more "spontaneous" may simply involve devising plans that recognize multiple paths to the same goal rather than one and only one path. Although it is a potential communicative virtue, "spontaneity" may not always produce appropriate communicative action and in fact may be considerably more plan-driven and less spontaneous than it appears to be at first blush.

CONCLUSION

A decade after the midpoint of the 20th century, Miller, Galanter, and Pribram (1960) introduced the plan concept into the lexicon of the behavioral sciences as a partial antidote to the then-rampant virus known as "behaviorism." Although this move was an important precursor to the subsequent cognitive revolution in the social sciences, it is important to keep in mind that simply invoking such mental predicates as "plan" or "script" to explain seemingly purposive behavior, including communicative action, begs many questions, especially without a fully articulated theory in which to embed the plan construct. In the absence of the requisite theoretical articulation, explaining goal-directed action by recourse to the plan construct alone degenerates into an exercise in hypostatization—explaining by mere labeling.

Although there is certainly no guarantee, perhaps the theory and research presented in this volume will enable us to avoid such counterproductive, cognitive cul-de-sacs and propel us down the road to more insightful ways of thinking about cognition and communication in general and message production processes in particular. As I hope I have been able to make clear in this volume, there are a number of exciting and interesting questions about message plans, message planning, and the production of communicative action yet to be addressed within the plan-based perspective presented here. I hope you have found these questions to be as challenging and intriguing as I have. Of course, I am certain that you will generate questions about message planning and social interaction that have yet to cross my mind.

References

$$\text{ᛒᛟ} \quad \blacklozenge \quad \text{ᚳᛃ}$$

Abbott, V. A., & Black, J. B. (1986). Goal-related inferences in comprehension. In J. A. Galambos, R. P. Abelson, & J. B. Black (Eds.), *Knowledge structures* (pp.123–142). Hillsdale, NJ: Lawrence Erlbaum Associates.

Allen, T. H., & Edwards, R. (1991, November). *The effects of imagined interaction and planning on speech fluency.* Paper presented at the annual conference of the Speech Communication Association, Chicago, IL.

Allen, T. H., & Honeycutt, J. M. (1996). *An analysis of the effects of imagined interactions and planning on the use of object adaptors.* Unpublished paper, Department of Speech Communication, Long Beach State University, Long Beach, CA.

Alterman, R. (1988). Adaptive planning. *Cognitive Science, 12,* 393–421.

Appelt, D. E. (1982). Planning natural-language utterances. In *Proceedings of the national conference on artificial intelligence* (pp. 59–62). Menlo Park, CA: American Association for Artificial Intelligence.

Appelt, D. E. (1985). *Planning English sentences.* Cambridge, England: Cambridge University Press.

Applegate, J. L. (1990). Constructs and communication: A pragmatic integration. In G. Neimeyer & R. Neimeyer (Eds.), *Advances in personal construct psychology* (Vol. 1, pp. 203–230). Greenwich, CT: JAI.

Bacon, F. (1975). *The advancement of learning: Book I.* (W. A. Armstrong, Ed.). London: Athlone Press. (Original work published 1605)

Bandura, A. (1971). *Psychological modeling: Conflicting theories.* Chicago: Aldine Atherton.

Bandura, A. (1977). *Social learning theory.* Englewood Cliffs, NJ: Prentice-Hall.

Bandura, A. (1986). *Social foundations of thought and action: A social cognitive approach.* Englewood Cliffs, NJ: Prentice-Hall.

Bandura, A., & Walters, R. H. (1963). *Social learning and personality development.* New York: Holt, Rinehart & Winston.

Battman, W. (1989). Planning as a method of stress prevention: Will it pay off? In C. D. Spielberger, I. G. Sarason, & J. Strelau (Eds.), *Stress and anxiety: Volume 12* (pp. 259–275). New York: Hemisphere Publications.

Baxter, L. A. (1979). Self-disclosure as a relationship disengagement strategy: An exploratory investigation. *Human Communication Research, 5,* 215–222.

Baxter, L. A., & Wilmot, W. W. (1984). Secret tests: Social strategies for acquiring information about the state of the relationship. *Human Communication Research, 11,* 171–201.

Bell, R. A., & Daly, J. A. (1984). The affinity-seeking function of communication. *Communication Monographs, 51*, 91–115.

Berger, C. R. (1979). Beyond initial interaction: Uncertainty, understanding, and the development of interpersonal relationships. In H. Giles & R. St. Clair (Eds.), *Language and social psychology* (pp. 122–144). Oxford, England: Basil Blackwell.

Berger, C. R. (1985). Social power and interpersonal communication. In M. L. Knapp & G. R. Miller (Eds.), *Handbook of interpersonal communication* (pp. 439–499). Newbury Park, CA: Sage.

Berger, C. R. (1987). Communicating under uncertainty. In M. E. Roloff & G. R. Miller (Eds.), *Interpersonal processes: New directions in communication research* (pp. 39–62). Newbury Park, CA: Sage.

Berger, C. R. (1988a). Planning, affect, and social action generation. In R. L. Donohew, H. Sypher, & E. T. Higgins (Eds.), *Communication social cognition and affect* (pp. 93–116). Hillsdale, NJ: Lawrence Erlbaum Associates.

Berger, C. R. (1988b). Uncertainty and information exchange in developing relationships. In S. W. Duck (Ed.), *Handbook of personal relationships* (pp. 239–255). Chichester: John Wiley.

Berger, C. R. (1988c, May). *Communication plans and communicative performance.* Paper presented at the annual conference of the International Communication Association, New Orleans, LA.

Berger, C. R. (1994). Power, dominance, and social interaction. In M. L. Knapp & G. R. Miller (Eds.), *Handbook of interpersonal communication* (2nd ed., pp. 450–507). Newbury Park, CA: Sage.

Berger, C. R. (1995a). A plan-based approach to strategic communication. In D. E. Hewes (Ed.), *The cognitive bases of interpersonal communication* (pp. 141–179). Hillsdale, NJ: Lawrence Erlbaum Associates.

Berger, C. R. (1995b). Inscrutable goals, uncertain plans, and the production of communicative action. In C. R. Berger & M. Burgoon (Eds.), *Communication and social influence processes* (pp. 1–28). East Lansing: Michigan State University Press.

Berger, C. R. (1997). Message production under uncertainty. In G. Phillipsen & T. L. Albrecht (Eds.), *Developing communication theories* (pp. 29–57). Albany: SUNY Press.

Berger, C. R., & Bell, R. A. (1988). Plans and the initiation of social relationships. *Human Communication Research, 15*, 217–235.

Berger, C. R., & Bradac, J. J. (1982). *Language and social knowledge: Uncertainty in interpersonal relations.* London: Edward Arnold.

Berger, C. R., & Calabrese, R. J. (1975). Some explorations in initial interaction and beyond: Toward a developmental theory of interpersonal communication. *Human Communication Research, 1*, 99–112.

Berger, C. R., & diBattista, P. (1992a). Information seeking and plan elaboration: What do you need to know to know what to do? *Communication Monographs, 59*, 368–387.

Berger, C. R., & diBattista, P. (1992b, November). *Adapting plans to failed communication goals.* Paper presented at the annual convention of the Speech Communication Association, Chicago, IL.

Berger, C. R., & diBattista, P. (1993). Communication failure and plan adaptation: If at first you don't succeed, say it louder and slower. *Communication Monographs, 60*, 220–238.

Berger, C. R., & Douglas, W. (1981). Studies in interpersonal epistemology III: Anticipated interaction, self-monitoring, and observational context selection. *Communication Monographs, 48*, 183–196.

Berger, C. R., & Gudykunst, W. B. (1991). Uncertainty and communication. In B. Dervin (Ed.), *Progress in communication sciences, Vol. X*, (pp. 21–66). Norwood, NJ: Ablex.

Berger, C. R., & Jordan, J. M. (1991, May). *Iterative planning and social action: Repairing failed plans*. Paper presented at the annual convention of the International Communication Association, Chicago, IL.

Berger, C. R., & Jordan, J. M. (1992). Planning sources, planning difficulty, and verbal fluency. *Communication Monographs, 59*, 130–149.

Berger, C. R., Karol, S. H., & Jordan, J. M. (1989). When a lot of knowledge is a dangerous thing: The debilitating effects of plan complexity on verbal fluency. *Human Communication Research, 16*, 91–119.

Berger, C. R., & Kellermann, K. A. (1983). To ask or not to ask: Is that a question? In R. N. Bostron (Ed.), *Communication yearbook 7* (pp. 342–368). Newbury Park, CA: Sage.

Berger, C. R., & Kellermann, K. (1989). Personal opacity and social information gathering: Explorations in strategic communication. *Communication Research, 16*, 314–351.

Berger, C. R., & Kellermann, K. (1994). Acquiring social information. In J. A. Daly & J. M. Wiemann (Eds.), *Strategic interpersonal communication* (pp. 1–31). Hillsdale, NJ: Lawrence Erlbaum Associates.

Berger, C. R., Knowlton, S. W., & Abrahams, M. F. (1996). The hierarchy principle in strategic communication. *Communication Theory, 6*, 111–142.

Berscheid, E. (1983). Emotion. In H. H. Kelley, E. Berscheid, A. Christensen, J. H. Harvey, T. L. Huston, G. Levinger, E. McLintock, L. A. Peplau, & D. R. Peterson (Eds.), *Close relationships* (pp. 110–168). San Francisco: Freeman.

Berscheid, E., Graziano, W., Monson, T., & Dermer, M. (1976). Outcome dependency: Attention, attribution, and attraction. *Journal of Personality and Social Psychology, 34*, 978–989.

Black, J. B., & Bower, G. H. (1979). Episodes as chunks in narrative memory. *Journal of Verbal Learning and Verbal Behavior, 18*, 309–318.

Black, J. B., & Bower, G. H. (1980). Story understanding as problem-solving. *Poetics, 9*, 223–250.

Black, J. B., Kay, D. S., & Soloway, E. M. (1987). Goal and plan knowledge representations: From stories to text editors and programs. In J. M. Carroll (Ed.), *Interfacing thought* (pp. 36–60). Cambridge, MA: MIT Press.

Boster, F. J., & Stiff, J. B. (1984). Compliance gaining message selection behavior. *Human Communication Research, 10*, 539–556.

Bower, G. H., Black, J. B., & Turner, T. J. (1979). Scripts in memory for text. *Cognitive Psychology, 11*, 177–220.

Brand, M. (1984) *Intending and acting: Toward a naturalized theory of action*. Cambridge, MA: MIT Press.

Bratman, M. E. (1987). *Intentions, plans, and practical reason*. Cambridge, MA: Harvard University Press.

Bratman, M. E. (1990). What is intention? In P. R. Cohen, J. Morgan, & M. E. Pollack (Eds.), *Intentions in communication* (pp. 15–31). Cambridge, MA: MIT Press.

Broadbent, D. E., Cooper, P. F., Fitzgerald, P., & Parkes, K. R. (1982). The cognitive failures questionnaire and its correlates. *British Journal of Clinical Psychology, 21*, 1–16.

Brown, P., & Levinson, S. (1978). Universals in language usage: Politeness phenomena. In E. Goody (Ed.), *Questions and politeness* (pp. 56–289). Cambridge, England: Cambridge University Press.

Brown, P., & Levinson, S. (1987). *Politeness: Some universals in language usage.* Cambridge, England: Cambridge University Press.

Bruce, B., & Newman, D. (1978). Interacting plans. *Cognitive Science, 2,* 195–233.

Burgoon, J. K., Birk, T., & Pfau, M. (1990). Nonverbal behaviors, persuasion, and credibility. *Human Communication Research, 17,* 140–169.

Burleson, B. R. (1987). Cognitive complexity. In J. C. McCroskey & J. A. Daly (Eds.), *Personality and interpersonal communication* (pp. 305–349). Newbury Park, CA: Sage.

Burleson, B. R. (1989). The constructivist approach to person-centered communication: Analysis of a research exemplar. In B. A. Dervin, L. Grossberg, B. J. O'Keefe, & E. Wartella (Eds.), *Rethinking communication, Vol. 2: Paradigm exemplars* (pp. 29–46). Newbury Park, CA: Sage.

Burleson, B. R. (1994). Comforting messages: Features, functions, and outcomes. In J. A. Daly & J. M. Wiemann (Eds.), *Strategic interpersonal communication* (pp. 135–161). Hillsdale, NJ: Lawrence Erlbaum Associates.

Butterworth, B. (1980). Evidence from pauses in speech. In B. Butterworth (Ed.), *Language production Volume 1: Speech and talk* (pp. 155–176). New York: Academic Press.

Butterworth, B., & Goldman-Eisler, F. (1979). Recent studies in cognitive rhythm. In A. W. Siegman & S. Feldstein (Eds.), *Of speech and time: Temporal speech patterns in interpersonal contexts* (pp. 211–224). Hillsdale, NJ: Lawrence Erlbaum Associates.

Cahill, A., & Mitchell, D. C. (1987). Plans and goals in story comprehension. In R. G. Reilly (Ed.), *Communication failure in dialogue and discourse* (pp. 257–268). New York; North-Holland.

Cappella, J. N. (1987). Interpersonal communication: Definitions and fundamental questions. In C. R. Berger & S. H. Chaffee (Eds.), *Handbook of communication science* (pp. 184–238). Newbury Park, CA: Sage.

Carberry, S. (1990). *Plan recognition in natural language dialogue.* Cambridge, MA: MIT Press.

Carbonell, J. G. (1981). Counterplanning: A strategy-based model of adversary planning in real-world situations. *Artificial Intelligence, 16,* 295–329.

Cegala, D. J., & Waldron, V. R. (1992). A study of the relationship between communication performance and conversation participant's thoughts. *Communication Studies, 43,* 105–125.

Christenfeld, N. (1994). Options and ums. *Journal of Language and Social Psychology, 13,* 192–199.

Christie, R., & Geis, F. L. (1970). *Studies in Machiavellianism.* New York: Academic Press.

Chomsky, N. (1965). *Aspects of the theory of syntax.* Cambridge, MA: MIT Press.

Clark, R. A. (1979). The impact of self interest and desire for liking on the selection of communication strategies. *Communication Monographs, 46,* 257–273.

Cody, M. J., Marston, P. J., & Foster, M. (1984). Deception: Paralinguistic and verbal leakage. In R. N. Bostrom (Ed.), *Communication yearbook 8* (pp. 464–490). Beverly Hills, CA: Sage.

Cody, M. J., Canary, D. J., & Smith, S. W. (1994). Compliance-gaining goals: An inductive analysis of actors' goal types, strategies, and success. In J. A. Daly & J. W. Wiemann (Eds.), *Strategic interpersonal communication* (pp. 33–90). Hillsdale, NJ: Lawrence Erlbaum Associates.

Cody, M. J., & McLaughlin, M. L. (Eds.). (1990). *The psychology of tactical communication*. Clevedon, England: Multilingual Matters.

Cody, M. J., McLaughlin, M. L., & Jordan, W. J. (1980). A multidimensional scaling of three sets of compliance-gaining strategies. *Communication Quarterly, 28,* 34–46.

Cody, M. J., McLaughlin, M. L., & Schneider, M. J. (1981). The impact of relational consequences and intimacy on the selection of interpersonal persuasion tactics: A reanalysis. *Communication Quarterly, 29,* 91–106.

Cohen, P. R., Morgan, J., & Pollack, M. E. (Eds.). (1990). *Intentions in communication.* Cambridge, MA: MIT Press.

Cohen, P. R., & Perrault, C. R. (1979). Elements of a plan-based theory of speech acts. *Cognitive Science, 3,* 177–212.

Cooley, C. H. (1902). *Human nature and the social order.* New York: Scribner's Sons.

Coombs, C. H. (1964). *A theory of data.* New York: Wiley.

Craig, R. T. (1989). Communication as a practical discipline. In B. Dervin, L. Grossberg, B. J. O'Keefe, & E. Wartella (Eds.), *Rethinking communication volume 1: Paradigm issues* (pp. 97–122). Newbury Park, CA: Sage.

D'Agostino, R. B. (1971). A second look at analysis of variance of dichotomous data. *Journal of Educational Measurement, 8,* 327–333.

Daly, J. A., & Kreiser, P. O. (1994). Affinity seeking. In J. A. Daly & J. M. Wiemann (Eds.), *Strategic interpersonal communication* (pp. 109–134). Hillsdale, NJ: Lawrence Erlbaum Associates.

Daly, J. A., & Wiemann, J. (Eds.). (1994). *Strategic interpersonal communication.* Hillsdale, NJ: Lawrence Erlbaum Associates.

Day, M. E. (1964). An eye movement phenomenon relating to attention, thought and anxiety. *Perceptual and Motor Skills, 19,* 443–446.

De Lisi, R. (1987). A cognitive-developmental model of planning. In S. L. Friedman, E. K. Scholnick, & R. R. Cocking (Eds.), *Blueprints for thinking: The role of planning in cognitive development* (pp. 79–109). Cambridge, England: Cambridge University Press.

Denton, W. H., Sprenkle, D. H., & Burleson, B. R. (1993, February). *The relationship of interpersonal cognitive complexity and communication performance in marriage: Moderating the effects of marital distress.* Paper presented at the annual conference of the Western Communication Association, Albuquerque, NM.

DePaulo, B. M., Davis, T., & Lanier, K. (1980, April). *Planning lies: The effects of spontaneity and arousal on success at deception.* Paper presented at the annual meeting of the Eastern Psychological Association, Hartford, CT.

deTurck, M. A. (1985). A transactional analysis of compliance-gaining behavior: Effects of noncompliance, relational contexts, and actor's gender. *Human Communication Research, 12,* 54–78.

deTurck, M. A. (1987). When communication fails: Physical aggression as a compliance-gaining strategy. *Communication Monographs, 54,* 106–112.

di Battista, P., & Abrahams, M. (1995). The role of relational information in the production of deceptive messages. *Communication Reports, 8,* 120–127.

Dillard, J. P. (1988). Compliance-gaining message-selection: What is our dependent variable? *Communication Monographs, 55,* 162–183.

Dillard, J. P. (Ed.) (1990a). *Seeking compliance, the production of interpersonal influence messages.* Scottsdale, AZ: Gorsuch Scarisbrick.

Dillard, J. P. (1990b). The nature and substance of goals in tactical communication. In M. J. Cody & M. L. McLaughlin (Eds.), *The psychology of tactical communication* (pp. 70–90). Clevedon, England: Multilingual Matters.

Dillard, J. P., & Burgoon, M. (1985). Situational influences on the selection of compli-ance-gaining messags: Two tests of the predictive utility of the Cody–McLaughlin typology. *Communication Monographs, 52,* 289–304.

Douglas, W. (1987). Affinity-testing in initial interactions. *Journal of Social and Personal Relationships, 4,* 3–15.

Edgar, T., Fitzpatrick, M. A., & Freimuth, V. S. (Eds.), (1992). *AIDS: A communication perspective* . Hillsdale, NJ: Lawrence Erlbaum Associates.

Edwards, R., Honeycutt, J., & Zagacki, K. S. (1988). Imagined interactions as an element of social cognition. *Western Journal of Speech Communication, 52,* 23–45.

Edwards, R., Honeycutt, J., & Zagacki, K. (1989). Sex differences in imagined interac-tion. *Sex Roles, 21,* 259–268.

Elliot, G. C. (1979). Some effects of deception and level of self-monitoring on planning and reacting to a self-presentation. *Journal of Personality and Social Psychology, 37,* 1282–1292.

Ericsson, K. A., & Simon, H. (1984) *Protocol analysis: Verbal reports as data.* Cambridge, MA: MIT Press.

Falbo, T. (1977). Multidimensional scaling of power strategies. *Journal of Personality and Social Psychology, 35,* 537–547.

Falbo, T., & Peplau, L. A. (1980). Power strategies in intimate relationships. *Journal of Personality and Social Psychology, 38,* 618–628.

Fiske, S. T., & Taylor, S. E. (1984). *Social cognition.* New York: Random House.

Fiske, S. T., & Taylor, S. E. (1991). *Social cognition.* (2nd ed.). New York: McGraw-Hill.

Frese, M., & Sabini, J. (Eds.) (1985). *Goal directed behavior: The concept of action in psychology.* Hillsdale, NJ: Lawrence Erlbaum Associates.

Galambos, J. A., Abelson, R. P., & Black, J. B. (1986). Goals and plans. In J. A. Galambos, R. P. Abelson, & J. B. Black (Eds.), *Knowledge structures* (pp. 101–102). Hillsdale, NJ: Lawrence Erlbaum Associates.

Gergen, K. J. (1985). The social constructionist movement in modern psychology. *American Psychologist, 40,* 266–275.

Goffman, E. (1959). *The presentation of self in everyday life.* Garden City, NY: Doubleday.

Goffman, E. (1969). *Strategic interaction.* Philadelphia: University of Pennsylvania Press.

Goodstadt, B. E., & Kipnis, D. (1970). Situational influences in the use of power. *Journal of Applied Psychology, 54,* 201–207.

Green, G. M. (1989). *Pragmatics and natural language understanding.* Hillsdale, NJ: Lawrence Erlbaum Associates.

Greenberg, B. S. (1974). Gratifications of television viewing and their correlates for British children. In J. G. Blumler & E. Katz (Eds.), *The uses of mass communication* (pp. 71–92). Beverly Hills, CA: Sage.

Greene, J. O. (1984a). Speech preparation processes and verbal fluency. *Human Com-munication Research, 11,* 61–84.

Greene, J. O. (1984b). A cognitive approach to human communication: An action assembly theory. *Communication Monographs, 51,* 289–306.

Greene, J. O. (1990). Tactical social actions: Towards some strategies for theory. In M. J. Cody & M. L. McLaughlin (Eds.), *The psychology of tactical communication* (pp. 31–47). Clevedon, England: Multilingual Matters.

Greene, J. O. (1995). An action-assembly perspective on verbal and nonverbal message production: A dancer's message unveiled. In D. E. Hewes (Ed.), *The cognitive bases of interpersonal communication* (pp. 51–85). Hillsdale, NJ: Lawrence Erlbaum Asso-ciates.

Green, J. O., & Geddes, D. (1993). An action assembly perspective on social skill. *Communication Theory, 3,* 26–49.

Greene, J. O., O'Hair, H. D., Cody, M. J., & Yen, C. (1985). Planning and control of behavior during deception. *Human Communication Research, 11,* 335–364.

Greenwald, A. G., Pratkanis, A. R., Leippe, M. R., & Baumgardner, M. H. (1986). Under what conditions does theory obstruct research progress? *Psychological Review, 93,* 216–229.

Guterman, S. S. (1970). *The Machiavellians.* Lincoln: University of Nebraska Press.

Hale, C. L., & Delia, J. G. (1976). Cognitive complexity and social perspective taking. *Communication Monographs, 43,* 195–203.

Hall, P. (1980). *Great planning disasters.* London: Weidenfeld & Nicolson.

Hammond, K.J. (1989a). *Case-based planning: Viewing planning as a memory task.* New York: Academic Press.

Hammond, K.J. (1989b). CHEF. In C. K. Riesbeck & R. C. Schank (Eds.), *Inside case-based reasoning* (pp.165–248). Hillsdale, NJ: Lawrence Erlbaum Associates.

Hayes-Roth, B. (1980). *Estimation of time requirements during planning: Interactions between motivation and cognition* (Rand Note N 1581–ONR). Santa Monica, CA: Rand Corporation.

Hayes-Roth, B., & Hayes-Roth, F. (1979). A cognitive model of planning. *Cognitive Science, 3,* 275–310.

Hermann, T. (1983). *Speech and situation: A psychological conception of situated speaking.* Berlin: Springer-Verlag.

Hewes, D. E. (1995). Cognitive processing of problematic messages: Reinterpreting to 'unbias' texts. In D. E. Hewes (Ed.), *The cognitive bases of interpersonal communication* (pp. 113–138). Hillsdale, NJ: Lawrence Erlbaum Associates.

Hewes, D. E., Graham, M. L. (1989). Second-guessing theory: Review and extension. In J. A. Anderson (Ed.), *Communication Yearbook 12* (pp. 213–248). Newbury Park, CA: Sage.

Hirokawa, R. Y., Mickey, J., & Miura, S. (1991). Effects of request legitimacy on the compliance-gaining tactics of male and female managers. *Communication Monographs, 58,* 421–436.

Hjelmquist, E. (1991). Planning and execution of discourse in conversation. *Communication and Cognition, 24,* 1–17.

Hjelmquist, E., & Gidlund, A. (1984). Planned ideas versus expressed ideas in conversation. *Journal of Pragmatics, 8,* 329–343.

Hobbs, J. R., & Evans, D. A. (1980). Conversation as planned behavior. *Cognitive Science, 4,* 349–377.

Hogarth, R. M. (1980). *Judgement and choice: The psychology of decision.* New York: Wiley.

Holloway, C. (1986). *Strategic planning.* Chicago: Nelson-Hall.

Honeycutt, J. M. (1989). A functional analysis of imagined interaction activity in everyday life. In J. E. Shorr, P. Robin, J. A. Connelia, & M. Wolpin (Eds.), *Imagery: Current perspectives* (pp. 13–25). New York: Plenum.

Honeycutt, J. M. (1991). Imagined interactions, imagery and mindfulness/mindlessness. In R. Kunzendorf (Ed.), *Mental imagery* (pp. 121–128). New York: Plenum.

Honeycutt, J. M., Edwards, R., & Zagacki, K. S. (1989–1990). Using imagined interaction features to predict measures of self-awareness: Loneliness, locus of control, self-dominance, and emotional intensity. *Imagination, Cognition and Personality, 9,* 17–31.

Honeycutt, J. M., Zagacki, K. S., & Edwards, R. (1992–1993). Imagined interaction, conversational sensitivity and communication competence. *Imagination, Cognition and Personality, 12,* 139–157.

Hovy, E. H. (1988). *Generating natural language under pragmatic constraints*. Hillsdale, NJ: Lawrence Erlbaum Associates.

Hovy, E. H. (1990). Pragmatics and natural language generation. *Artificial Intelligence, 43*, 153–197.

Hunter, J. E., & Boster, F. J. (1987). A model of compliance-gaining message selection. *Communication Monographs, 54*, 63–84.

Ickes, W., Robertson, E., Took, W., & Teng, G. (1986). Naturalistic social cognition: Methodology, assessment, and validation. *Journal of Personality and Social Psychology, 51*, 66–82.

Instone, D., Major, B., & Bunker, B. B. (1983). Gender, self-confidence, and social influence strategies: An organizational simulation. *Journal of Personality and Social Psychology, 44*, 322–333.

Janis, I. L., & Mann, L. (1977). *Decision making: A psychological analysis of conflict, choice, and commitment*. New York: Free Press.

Jones, E. E. (1964). *Ingratiation: A social psychological analysis*. New York: Appelton-Century-Crofts.

Jones, E. E., & Davis, K. E. (1965). From acts to dispositions: The attribution process in person perception. In L. Berkowitz (Ed.), *Advances in experimental social psychology* (pp. 219–266). New York: Academic Press.

Jones, E. E., & Wortman, C. (1973). *Ingratiation: An attributional approach*. Morristown, NJ: General Learning Press.

Jordan, J. M. (1993). *An exploration of executive control processes in conversations: Extending a plan-based model of communication*. Unpublished doctoral dissertation, Department of Communication Studies, Northwestern University, Evanston, IL.

Jordan, J. M., & Roloff, M. E. (1995). *Planning skills and negotiator goal attainment: The relationship between self-monitoring and plan generation, plan enactment and plan consequences*. Unpublished paper, Department of Communication, University of Cincinnati, Cincinnati, OH.

Kahneman, D., Slovic, P., & Tversky, A. (1982). *Judgment under uncertainty: Heuristics and biases*. New York: Cambridge University Press.

Kaminski, E. P., McDermott, S. T., & Boster, F. J. (1977, April). *The use of compliance-gaining strategies as a function of Machiavellianism and situation*. Paper presented at the annual convention of the Central States Speech Association, Southfield, MI.

Katz, E., Blumler, J. G., & Gurevitch, M. (1974). Utilization of mass communication by the individual. In J. G. Blumler & E. Katz (Eds.), *The uses of mass communication* (pp. 19–32). Beverly Hills, CA: Sage.

Kellermann, K. (1991). The conversation MOP II: Progression through scenes in discourse. *Human Communication Research, 17*, 385–414.

Kellermann, K. (1992). Communication: Inherently strategic and primarily automatic. *Communication Monographs, 59*, 288–300.

Kellermann, K. (1995). The conversation MOP: A model of patterned and pliable behavior. In D. E. Hewes (Ed.), *Cognitive bases of interpersonal communication* (pp. 181–221). Hillsdale, NJ: Lawrence Erlbaum Associates.

Kellermann, K. A., & Berger, C. R. (1984). Affect and the acquisition of social information: Sit back, relax, and tell me about yourself. In R. Bostrom (Ed.), *Communication yearbook 8* (pp. 412–445). Newbury Park, CA: Sage.

Kellermann, K., Broetzmann, S., Lim, T., & Kitao, K. (1989). The conversation MOP: Scenes in the stream of discourse. *Discourse Processes, 12*, 27–62.

Kellermann, K., & Cole, T. (1994). Classifying compliance gaining messages: Taxonomic disorder and strategic confusion. *Communication Theory, 4*, 3–60.

Kellermann, K., & Lim, T. (1990). The conversation MOP: III. Timing scenes in discourse. *Journal of Personality and Social Psychology, 59*, 1163–1179.

Kelly, G. A. (1955). *The psychology of personal constructs.* New York: Norton.

Kipnis, D., & Consentino, J. (1969). Use of leadership powers in industry. *Journal of Applied Psychology, 53*, 460–466.

Kirk, R. E. (1968). *Experimental design: Procedures for the behavioral sciences.* Belmont, CA: Wadsworth.

Knapp, M. L., & Hall, J. A. (1992). *Nonverbal communication in human interaction.* (3rd edition). Fort Worth: Holt, Rinehart & Winston.

Knowlton, S. W. (1994). *The hierarchy hypothesis and planning alternatives.* Unpublished thesis, Department of Rhetoric and Communication, University of California, Davis.

Knowlton, S. W., & Berger, C. R. (in press). Message planning, communication failure, and cognitive load: Further explorations of the hierarchy principle. *Human Communication Research.*

Kreitler, S., & Kreitler, H. (1987). Plans and planning: Their motivational and cognitive antecedents. In S. L. Friedman, E. K. Skolnick, & R. R. Cocking (Eds.), *Blueprints for thinking: The role of planning in cognitive development* (pp. 110–178). New York: Cambridge University Press.

Kuhl, J., & Beckman, J. (Eds.) (1985). *Action control: From cognition to behavior.* New York: Springer-Verlag.

Kunda, Z., & Nisbett, R. (1986). The psychometrics of everyday life. *Cognitive Psychology, 18*, 195–224.

Langer, E. J. (1978). Rethinking the role of thought in social interaction. In J. H. Harvey, W. Ickes, & R. F. Kidd (Eds.), *New directions in attribution research: Volume 2* (pp. 3–58). New York: Wiley.

Langer, E. (1992). Interpersonal mindlessness and language. *Communication Monographs, 59*, 324–327.

Larson, G. E., & Merritt, C. R. (1991). Can accidents be predicted? An empirical test of the Cognitive Failures Questionnaire. *Applied Psychology: An International Review, 40*, 37–45.

Lennox, R. D., & Wolfe, R. N. (1984). Revision of the self-monitoring scale. *Journal of Personality and Social Psychology, 46*, 1349–1364.

Levelt, W. J. M. (1989). *Speaking: From intention to articulation.* Cambridge, MA: MIT Press.

Levison, S. (1981). Some preobservations on the modelling of dialogue. *Discourse Processes, 4*, 93–116.

Lewicki, P. (1986). *Nonconscious social information processing.* Orlando, FL: Academic Press.

Lichtenstein, E. H., & Brewer, W. F. (1980). Memory for goal directed events. *Cognitive Psychology, 12*, 412–445.

Litman, D., & Allen, J. (1987). A plan recognition model for subdialogues in conversation. *Cognitive Science, 11*, 163–200.

Littlepage, G. E., & Pineault, M. A. (1982). *Detection of deception of planned and spontaneous communications.* Unpublished paper, Department of Psychology, Middle Tennessee State University, Murfreesboro, TN.

Livingston, K. R. (1980). Love as a process of uncertainty reduction-cognitive theory. In K. S. Pope and Associates, *On love and loving* (pp. 133–151). San Francisco: Jossey-Bass.

Longhurst, T. M., & Siegel, G. M. (1973). Effects of communication failure on speaker and listener behavior. *Journal of Speech and Hearing Research, 16,* 128–140.

Mandler, G. (1975). *Mind and emotion.* New York: Wiley.

Marwell, G., & Schmitt, D. R. (1967). Dimensions of compliance-gaining behavior: An empirical analysis. *Sociometry, 30,* 350–364.

McCann, C. D., & Higgins, E. T. (1988). Motivation and affect in interpersonal relations: The role of personal orientations and discrepancies. In L. Donohew, H. E. Sypher, & E. T. Higgins (Eds), *Communication, social cognition, and affect* (pp. 53–79). Hillsdale, NJ: Lawrence Erlbaum Associates.

McQuail, D. (1987). Functions of communication: A nonfunctionalist overview. In C. R. Berger & S. H. Chaffee (Eds.), *Handbook of Communication Science* (pp. 327–349). Newbury Park, CA: Sage.

Mead, G. H. (1934). *Mind, self and society: From the standpoint of a social behaviorist.* Chicago: University of Chicago Press.

Metts, S., & Fitzpatrick, M. A. (1992). Thinking about safer sex: The risky business of "know your partner" advice. In T. Edgar, M. A. Fitzpatrick, & V. S. Freimuth (Eds.), *AIDS: A communication perspective* (pp. 1–19). Hillsdale, NJ: Lawrence Erlbaum Associates.

Miller, G. A., Galanter, E., & Pribram, K. H. (1960). *Plans and the structure of behavior.* New York: Holt, Rinehart, & Winston.

Miller, G. R. (1987). Persuasion. In C. R. Berger & S. H. Chaffee (Eds.), *Handbook of communication science* (pp. 446–483). Newbury Park, CA: Sage.

Miller, G. R., Boster, F. J., Roloff, M. E., & Seibold, D. R. (1977). Compliance-gaining message strategies: A topology and some findings concerning effects of situational differences. *Communication Monographs, 44,* 37–51.

Miller, G. R., Boster, F. J., Roloff, M. E., & Seibold, D. R. (1987). MBRS rekindled: Some thoughts on compliance gaining in interpersonal settings. In M. E. Roloff & G. R. Miller (Eds.), *Interpersonal processes: New directions in communication research* (pp. 89–116). Newbury Park, CA: Sage.

Miller, G. R., deTurck, M. A., & Kalbfleisch, P. J. (1983). Self-monitoring, rehearsal, and deceptive communication. *Human Communication Research, 10,* 97–117.

Miller, G. R., & Hewgill, M. A. (1964). The effect of variations in nonfluency on audience ratings of source credibility. *Quarterly Journal of Speech, 50,* 36–44.

Miller, G. R., & Stiff, J. B. (1993). *Deceptive communication.* Newbury Park, CA: Sage.

Newell, K. M. (1978). Some issues in action plans. In G. E. Stelmach (Ed.), *Information processing in motor control and learning* (pp. 41–54). New York: Academic Press.

Nisbett, R. E., & Ross, L. (1980). *Human inference: Strategies and shortcomings of social judgment.* Englewood Cliffs, NJ: Prentice-Hall.

Nisbett, R. E., & Wilson, T. D. (1977). Telling more than we can know: Verbal reports on mental processes. *Psychological Review, 84,* 231–259.

Norman, D. A. (1981). Categorization of action slips. *Psychological Review, 88,* 1–15.

Nuttin, J. (1984). *Motivation, planning and action.* Hillsdale, NJ: Lawrence Erlbaum Associates.

O'Keefe, B. J. (1988). The logic of message design: Individual differences in reasoning about communication. *Communication Monographs, 55,* 80–103.

O'Keefe, B. J. (1997). Variation, adaptation, and functional explanation in the study of message design. In G. Phillipsen & T. Albrecht (Eds.), *Developing communication theories* (pp. 85–118). Albany: State University of New York Press.

O'Keefe, B. J., & Delia, J. G. (1982). Impression formation and message production. In M. E. Roloff & C. R. Berger (Eds.), *Social cognition and communication* (pp. 33–72). Beverly Hills, CA: Sage.

O'Keefe, B. J., & Lambert, B. L. (1995). Managing the flow of ideas: A local management approach to message design. In B. R. Burleson (Ed.), *Communication yearbook 18* (pp. 54–82). Newbury Park, CA: Sage.

O'Keefe, B. J., & McCornack, S. A. (1987). Message design logic and message goal structure: Effects on perceptions of messages. *Human Communication Research, 14,* 68–92.

O'Keefe, B. J., & Shepard, G. J. (1987). The pursuit of multiple objectives in face-to-face persuasive interactions: Effects of construct differentiation on message organization. *Communication Monographs, 54,* 396–419.

Owens, J., Bower, G. H., & Black, J. B. (1979). The "soap opera" effect in story recall. *Memory and Cognition, 7,* 185–191.

Palmgreen, P., Rosengren, K. E., & Wenner, L. A. (Eds.). (1985). *Media gratification research: Current perspectives.* Newbury Park, CA: Sage.

Patterson, M. L. (1983). *Nonverbal behavior: A functional perspective.* New York: Springer-Verlag.

Patterson, M. L. (1995). A parallel process model of nonverbal communication. *Journal of Nonverbal Behavior, 19,* 3–29.

Patterson, M. L. (in press). Social behavior and social cognition: A parallel process approach. In J. L. Nye & M. Brower (Eds.), *What's social about social cognition? Social cognition research in small groups.* Thousand Oaks, CA: Sage.

Patterson, M. L., Churchill, M. E., Farag, F., & Borden, E. (1991–92). Impression management, cognitive demand, and interpersonal sensitivity. *Current Pyschology: Research and Reviews, 10,* 263–271.

Pea, R. D., & Hawkins, J. (1987). Planning in a chore-scheduling task. In S. L. Friedman, E. K. Skolnick, & R. R. Cocking (Eds.), *Blueprints for thinking: The role of planning in cognitive development* (pp. 273–302). New York: Cambridge University Press.

Perrault, R., & Allen, J. (1980). A plan-based analysis of indirect speech acts. *American Journal of Computational Linguistics, 6,* 167–182.

Pervin, L. A. (Ed.) (1989). *Goal concepts in personality and social psychology.* Hillsdale, NJ: Lawrence Erlbaum Associates.

Petty, R. E., & Cacioppo, J. T. (1981). *Attitudes and persuasion—classic and contemporary approaches.* Dubuque, IA : W. C. Brown.

Petty, R. E., & Cacioppo, J. T. (1986). *Communication and persuasion: Central and peripheral routes to attitude change.* New York: Springer-Verlag.

Popper, K. R. (1969). *Conjectures and refutations: The growth of scientific knowledge* (3rd Edition). London: Routledge & Paul.

Posner, M. I., & Snyder, C. R. R. (1975). Attention and cognitive control. In R. L. Solso, (Ed.), *Information processing and cognition: The Loyola Symposium* (pp. 55–85). Hillsdale, NJ: Lawrence Erlbaum Associates.

Read, S. J., & Miller, L. C. (1989). Inter-personalism: Toward a goal-based theory of persons in relationships. In L. A. Pervin (Ed.), *Goal concepts in personality and social psychology* (pp. 413–472). Hillsdale, NJ: Lawrence Erlbaum Associates.

Reason, J. T. (1990). *Human error.* New York: Cambridge University Press.

Riesbeck, C. K. & Schank, R. C. (1989). *Inside case-based reasoning*. Hillsdale, NJ: Lawrence Erlbaum Associates.

Ringle, M. H., & Bruce, B. C. (1980). Conversation failure. In W. G. Lehnert & M. H. Ringle (Eds.), *Strategies for natural language processing* (pp. 203–221). Hillsdale, NJ: Lawrence Erlbaum Associates.

Roloff, M. E., & Barnicott, Jr., E. F. (1978). The situational use of pro- and anti-social compliance-gaining strategies by high and low machiavellians. In B. D. Rubin (Ed.), *Communication yearbook 2* (pp. 193–205). New Brunswick, NJ: Transaction Books.

Roloff, M. E., & Barnicott, Jr., E. F. (1979). The influence of dogmatism on the situational use of pro- and anti-social compliance-gaining strategies. *Southern Speech Communication Journal, 45,* 37–54.

Rokeach, M. (1968). *Beliefs, attitudes, and values; a theory of organization and change.* San Francisco: Jossey-Bass.

Rokeach, M. (1973). *The nature of human values.* New York: Free Press.

Rule, B. G., & Bisanz, G. L. (1987). Goals and strategies of persuasion: A cognitive schema for understanding social events. In M. P. Zanna, J. M. Olson, & C. P. Herman (Eds.), *Social influence: The Ontario symposium Vol. 5* (pp. 185–206). Hillsdale, NJ: Lawrence Erlbaum Associates.

Rule, B. G., Bisanz, G. L., & Kohn, M. (1985). Anatomy of a persuasion schema: Targets, goals, and strategies. *Journal of Personality and Social Psychology, 48,* 1127–1140.

Russell, D. (1982). The measurement of loneliness. In L.A. Peplau & D. Perlman (Eds.), *Loneliness: A sourcebook of current theory, research and therapy* (pp. 81–104). New York: Wiley.

Russell, D., Peplau, L. A., & Cutrona, C. E. (1980). The revised UCLA loneliness scale: Concurrent and discrimminant validity evidence. *Journal of Personality and Social Psychology, 39,* 472–480.

Sacerdoti, E. (1977). *A structure for plans and behavior.* Amsterdam: Elsvier.

Saeki, M., & O'Keefe, B. J. (1994). Refusals and rejections: Designing messages to serve multiple goals. *Human Communication Research, 21,* 67–102.

Schachter, S. (1959). *The psychology of affiliation: Experimental studies of the sources of gregariousness.* Stanford, CA: Stanford University Press.

Schachter, S., Christenfeld, N., Ravina, B., & Bilous, F. (1991). Speech disfluency and the structure of knowledge. *Journal of Personality and Social Psychology, 60,* 362–367.

Schank, R. C. (1982). *Dynamic memory: A theory of reminding in computers and people.* New York: Cambridge University Press.

Schank, R. C. (1986). *Explanation patterns: Understanding mechanically and creatively.* Hillsdale, NJ: Lawrence Erlbaum Associates.

Schank, R. C., & Abelson, R. P. (1977). *Scripts, plans, goals and understanding.* Hillsdale, NJ: Lawrence Erlbaum Associates.

Schenk-Hamlin, W. J., Wiseman, R. L., & Georgacarakos, G. N. (1982). A model of properties of compliance-gaining strategies. *Communication Quarterly, 30,* 92–99.

Schmidt, C. F. (1976). Understanding human action: Recognizing the plans and motives of other persons. In J. S. Carroll, & J. W. Payne (Eds.), *Cognition and social behavior* (pp. 47–67). Hillsdale, NJ: Lawrence Erlbaum Associates.

Schneider, W., & Shiffrin, R. M. (1977). Controlled and automatic human information processing: 1. Detection, search, and attention. *Psychological Review, 84,* 1–66.

Seifert, C. M., Robertson, S. P., & Black, J. B. (1985). Types of inferences generated during reading. *Journal of Memory and Language, 24,* 405–422.

Sellars, W. (1966). Thought and action. In K. Lehrer (Ed.), *Freedom and determinism* (pp. 141–174). New York: Random House.

Sherman, S. J., & Corty, E. (1984). Cognitive heuristics. In R. S. Wyer, Jr. & T. K. Srull (Eds.), *Handbook of social cognition, Vol. 1* (pp. 189–286). Hillsdale, NJ: Lawrence Erlbaum Associates.

Shriffrin, R. M., & Schneider, W. (1977). Controlled and automatic information processing: II. Perceptual learning, automatic attending and a general theory. *Psychological Review, 84*, 127–190.

Siegler, R. S., & Jenkins, E. (1989). *How children discover new strategies*. Hillsdale, NJ: Lawrence Erlbaum Associates.

Sillars, A. L. (1980). The stranger and the spouse as target persons for compliance-gaining strategies: A subjective expected utility model. *Human Communication Research, 6*, 265-279.

Sillince, J. (1986). *A theory of planning*. Brookfield, VT: Gower.

Simon, H. A. (1955). A behavioral model of rational choice. *Quarterly Journal of Economics, 69*, 99-118.

Simon, H. A. (1956). Rational choice and the structure of the environment. *Psychological Review, 63*, 129–138.

Skinner, B. F. (1953). *Science and human behavior*. New York: Macmillan.

Snyder, M. (1974). Self-monitoring of expressive behavior. *Journal of Personality and Social Psychology, 30*, 526–537.

Snyder, M. (1987). *Public appearances/private realities*. New York: Freeman.

Srull, T. K., & Wyer, R. S. (1986). The role of chronic and temporary goals in social information processing. In R. Sorrentino & E. T. Higgins (Eds.), *Handbook of motivation and cognition* (pp. 503–549). New York: Guilford.

Sternberg, R. J. (1986). A triangular theory of love. *Psychological Review, 93*, 119–135.

Tracy, K., & Coupland, N. (Eds.) (1990). *Multiple goals in discourse*. Clevedon, England: Multilingual Matters.

Tracy, K., & Moran, J. P. (1983). Conversational relevance in multiple-goal settings. In R. T. Craig & K. Tracy (Eds.), *Conversational coherence: Form, structure, and strategy* (pp. 116–135). Beverly Hills, CA: Sage.

Uleman, J. S., & Bargh, J. A. (Eds.) (1989). *Unintended thought*. New York: Guilford.

Vallacher, R. R., & Wegner, D. M. (1985). *A theory of action identification*. Hillsdale, NJ: Lawrence Erlbaum Associates.

Vallacher, R. R., Wegner, D. M., & Somoza, M. (1989). That's easy for you to say: Action identification and speech fluency. *Journal of Personality and Social Psychology, 56*, 199–208.

vanDijk, T., & Kintsch, W. (1983). *Strategies of discourse comprehension*. New York: Academic Press.

Varonis, E. M., & Gass, S. M. (1985). Miscommunication in native/nonnative conversation. *Language in Society, 14*, 327–343.

von Cranach, M., Kalbermatten, U., Indermuhle, K., & Gugler, B. (1982). *Goal-directed action*. London: Academic Press.

Waldron, V. R. (1990). Constrained rationality: Situational influences on information acquisition plans and tactics. *Communication Monographs, 57*, 184–201.

Waldron, V. R., & Applegate, J. L. (1994). Interpersonal construct differentiation and conversational planning: An examination of two cognitive accounts for the production of competent verbal disagreement tactics. *Human Communication Research, 21*, 3–35.

Waldron, V. R., Caughlin, J. , & Jackson, D. (1995). Talking specifics: Facilitating effects of planning on AIDS talk in peer dyads. *Health Communication, 7*, 249–266.

Waldron, V. R., Cegala, D. J., Sharkey, W. F., & Teboul, B. (1990). Cognitive and tactical dimensions of goal management. *Journal of Language and Social Psychology, 9*, 101–118.

Watson, J. B. (1924). *Psychology, from the standpoint of a behaviorist.* Philadelphia: J. B. Lippincott.

Wheeless, L. R., Barraclough, R., & Stewart, R. (1983). Compliance-gaining and power in persuasion. In R. N. Bostrom (Ed.), *Communication Yearbook 7* (pp. 105–145). Newbury Park, CA: Sage.

Wiemann, J. M. (1977). Explication and test of a model of communicative competence. *Human Communication Research, 3*, 195–213.

Wilensky, R. (1983). *Planning and understanding: A computational approach to human reasoning.* Reading, MA: Addison-Wesley.

Wilson, T. D. (1994). The proper protocol: Validity and completeness of verbal reports. *Psychological Science, 5*, 249–252.

Winer, B. J. (1971). *Statistical principles in experimental design.* New York: McGraw-Hill.

Author Index

 ⁣

Subject Index

∽ ◆ ∾

Printed and bound by CPI Group (UK) Ltd, Croydon, CR0 4YY

28/10/2024

01780164-0002